# Prayer Tool

Armani D. White

# Prayer Tool

# &

# Prayer Tool Index

Includes 50+ divinely inspired prayers

# Copyright Page

*Prayer Tool*

Written by Armani White

Copyright © 2020 by Armani White.

All Rights Reserved.

Published by Rise Ministry, Inc.'s Publishing Group

ISBN: 978-1-7351105-0-9

Printed in the United States of America.

All rights reserved. No part of this publication may be reproduced, stored in a retrieval system, or transmitted in any form or by any means – electronic, mechanical, photocopy, recording, scanning or otherwise – without the prior written consent of the publisher, except by provided by the United States of America copyright law. Scripture quotations are taken from the New King James Version®. ©1982 by Thomas Nelson. They are used with permission.

Cover Design: Armani D. White

## Table of Contents

Dedication .................................................................. vii

Introduction ................................................................ ix

1. The Essence of a Prayer ........................... 13
2. Heart Posture ............................................. 25
3. Spirit of Worship ........................................ 35
4. Tongues of Worship .................................. 49
5. Prayers That Breaks the Yoke ................. 65
6. Prayers That Break the Powers .............. 79
7. Declare, and it shall be ............................ 91
8. Intercessors Arise .................................... 107

Prayer Tool Index .................................................... 123

Closing Declaration ................................................ 159

Salvation Prayer ...................................................... 161

*Armani D. White*

## *Dedication*

To the one who desires to know more of God. To the one who is patiently waiting for answered prayers. To the one who is up in the late-night hour, praying. To the one who desires to see God's will magnified upon the earth. KEEP PRAYING. God sees your heart, and He hears your prayers!

# Introduction

*H*ave you ever prayed and received *a suddenly*? Suddenly God answered? Suddenly God moved? Suddenly a breakthrough? God desperately wants to create a suddenly within the lives of His people. God is looking for a generation of people who are hungry for His blessings on their lives. Even more, God intends to surpass all of our expectations. But, the question is, *who is prepared for the move of God?*

The Word of God, in Matthew 7, tells us that if we ask, it will be given. If we seek, then we will find. If we knock, then the door will be opened.

And, by the Blood of Jesus, we are God's children, and we have full permission to access our Father. We must open our mouths

## Introduction

in prayer and seek the heart of our Lord. We must have audacity through the Holy Ghost to boldly yet humbly ask the Father to move on our behalf.

As co-heirs of the Kingdom of Heaven, it's our blood-bought right to ask anything in Jesus' name. As we ask, according to God's Word in John 14:14, Jesus will answer.

However, if we have free access to the Kingdom of Heaven through Jesus Christ, then why is that many of us are stagnant? We're stuck in our same ol' lifestyle: bound by sin, and afraid of the Father, believing He's an angry God. If Jesus promised to answer our prayers, then why are there unfilled and un-answered prayers.

We need answers. We cannot be stagnant. We have the power of Jesus on our side. Therefore, the days of passive Christianity are over. It's time to rise up, take our rightful position, and posture our hearts before the Lord. It's time to press deeper into the dimensions of the Spirit of God with a bold and fierce hunger.

It's time to pray more than ever! God is waiting for us. So, we must stand alongside Heaven. We must walk courageously, expecting God to move. Now is the time to press into a new dimension of prayer. Now is the time for fervent intercession. Now is the time to soar in worship.

God hungers to move among His people. Therefore, if we expect God to move, we must get into proper alignment with Heaven.

We must go into Heaven's treasure chest, pull out our Sword, and PRAY!

Child of God, the days of misappropriating your Prayer Tools are over! You need to use your prayer tools properly. Therefore, as you turn the pages of 'Prayer Tool,' you'll be immersed in the presence of God. Watch as He instructs, encourages you, and guides you to become a powerful and fervent man or woman of prayer who prays alongside Heaven.

Chapter | 1

## The Essence of a Prayer

Your prayers have the power to trigger the heartbeat of God. Your prayers, cries, and petitions really matter to our Lord. They matter because, when you pray, you are communicating in the number one language of Heaven. All of Heaven responds to an authentic, genuine, heartfelt, God-led prayer.

The importance of prayer is so extreme that God instructed us to pray without ceasing. In addition, God gives a powerful outline of how we ought to pray. Our guideline for prayer is modeled in Matthew 6:5-15. It's imperative that we consider our outline for prayer. As we lean into God's blueprint we'll become better equipped to feel the heartbeat of Jesus.

*And when you pray, you shall not be like the hypocrites...*

The Lord's prayer starts with, "And when you pray, you shall not be like the hypocrites. For they love to pray standing in the synagogues and on the corners of the streets, that they may be seen by men. Assuredly, I say to you, they have their reward" Matthew 6:5. I think it's important to note that God gives us a demonstration of what 'not' to do while praying. We shouldn't pray like the hypocrites, to be 'seen' as in a prideful way. Nor should we "use vain repetitions as the heathens do. For they think that they will be heard for their many words" Matthew 6:7.

The hearts of the *hypocrites* and *heathens* have been fashioned in such a way that they proclaimed the intentions of God, even though their hearts were far from Him.

They used elegant words and elaborate phrases that alluded to a 'higher ranking in religion.' Their true desires were hidden behind their pomps and pious appearances; they wanted to be seen and heard by men. They took pride in looking astute and cared more about their fame than God's ultimate objective.

Nonetheless, John 4:24 tells us that "God *is* Spirit, and those who worship Him must worship in spirit and truth." It's no wonder why they were called hypocrites and heathens. They weren't genuinely surrendered in prayer.

*But you, when you pray ...*

However, it's not enough to show and tell someone what not to do. For every list of don'ts, there should be a list of dos. Without a blueprint or a sense of direction, you'll naturally gravitate towards the path which you should've avoided. Therefore, when you "pray, go into your room, and when you have shut your door, pray to your Father who is in the secret place; and your Father who sees in secret will reward you openly" Matthew 6:6.

At this point, I think it's essential to establish that Jesus is not telling us that we shouldn't have corporate prayer. Since Acts 2 shows us that the disciples were gathered in corporate prayer when the Holy Spirit fell on them, how could it be wrong? Instead, Matthew 6:6 is referring to your personal prayer, the kind that happens in your *secret place*.

Your secret place is where you have an intimate and divine connection with the Father. This place must remain sacred as it's your quiet place, the place where you seek and commune with the Lord.

Like God told Moses in Exodus 3:5, your quiet place is the place where Holy Grounds are formed between you and our Savior. Because your secret place deals with the content of your heart, it shouldn't be created the moment you choose to have 'corporate prayer.' Instead, your secret place should have already been established between you and the Lord even before you show up for cooperate prayer. Public prayer is simply an accessory to the relationship you have with the Father, not the entree.

Therefore, how does your secret place look? Do you desire to have an intimate relationship with the Father? Are you seeking the Lord in prayer because you have a need, or are you seeking the Lord in prayer because you have considered His heart and desired His ways?

As a child of God who desires to seek and fulfill God's will, you're aware that "your Father knows the things you are in need of before you ask of Him" Matthew 6:8. Your awareness is not by hap chance, but rather from a place of security that can only be formed from your personal relationship with God. So, when entering prayer, enter from a holy and sovereign communion with the Father. Remember to always consider His directions and honor His Name.

**In this manner, therefore, pray...**

God gave us our blueprint to prayer so that we can learn how to build our relationship with God. We build our relationship with God, with an understanding of how to come before Him properly. God is holy and should be addressed accordingly.

"In this manner, therefore, pray Our Father in Heaven, hallowed be Your name. Your kingdom come. Your will be done on earth as it is in Heaven. Give us this day our daily bread. And forgive us our debts, as we forgive our debtors. And do not lead us into temptation, but deliver us from the evil one. For Yours is the kingdom and the power and the glory forever. Amen. Matthew 6:9-13

Most of us were raised to acknowledge and properly greet the residents of any home we enter. Walking into someone's home without this proper greeting is considered rude and disrespectful. The same is true with God.

Imagine being bombarded with a host of questions, concerns, and requests without even being greeted with a simple 'hello, how are you?' How motivated would you be to act in favor of their request?

Hence, the foundation of prayer begins with a greeting and acknowledgment of who God is. The name of our Father in Heaven should be hollowed, reverenced, and recognized for His sovereignty and His Great Name. Though God may answer prayers that don't begin with praises and acknowledgment, yet I wonder what our worship and God's response would be like if we just lavished Him with all our glory and admiration before any request or petition.

I can only imagine what type of mountains will be moved if we blessed the name of the Lord at all times, if we remember to honor Him in prayer.

For instance, if we simply enter God's gates with a 'Lord, You are good. Father, You are holy, and there is none like You.' Or even,

'Our Father in heaven, hallowed be Your name.' 'Father, You are worthy and worthy of being praised.'

And, if we simply bless the Lord and give Him our praise and worship without strings attached, how many mountains will move? God is a good Father, and He longs for a generation who will honor and love Him simply because HE IS.

## *Your kingdom come ...*

Did you know that prayer is a two-way communication device where both you and God are speaking and listening at the same time? Prayer can be considered as Heaven's telephone. However, most of the time, when we enter prayer, there's more request and delivery of wants versus getting down to *"God, what is Your will"?* There's more talking and less listening.

Nonetheless, the next verse, verse 10 of the Lord's prayer, addressed a genuine concern for God's heart. "Your kingdom come. Your will be done on earth as *it is* in Heaven," is a heart's posture that is more concerned about the manifestation of God's will than your desires and needs. This is merely asking God to bring His purposes into your life and this world.

Therefore, after you worship and praise, ask God for His purpose. 'Lord, what are Your plans concerning my life?' 'Lord, what are Your desire concerning this nation?' 'Father, I want to see Your will done on earth as it is in Heaven.' As you continue to mature in prayer and faith, you'll understand the magnitude of leading a life of God's will. When walking according to the ways of the Lord, you create an abundance of perpetual blessings.

However, please note that having abundant 'blessings' does not mean that everything will seamlessly happen as you wish. More importantly, divine blessings will usher you into the gates of God's eternal grace over your life, according to God's will. Now, what better way is there to live than to live under the sovereignty of the Father?

There is absolutely nothing better than God's will for your life. Though you may have your wants, dreams, and desires, remain encouraged. As you continue to walk a life in God's direction and favor, your desires are going to align with the Father's. When your desires are in agreement with God's plan, you'll confidently pray, 'Your will be done' because God's will have become yours. Welcome to the place of surrender.

### *Give us this day our Daily Bread*

Early in Jesus' walk of Ministry, The Holy Spirit led Him into the wilderness for forty days and forty nights to fast and pray. Just like any other time of praying and fasting, Jesus' assignment was to seek the Lord, fill up on His Word, and allow the Holy Spirit to continue to endow Him. However, after His time of devotion, the devil antagonized Him as per the continuum of the assignment.

*Prayer Tool*

Satan began taking jabs at Jesus' God-Head nature. The enemy tried to get our Lord to stoop to his level by prematurely doing signs and miracles. What if Jesus obliged to do such wonders? Yes, if He did, Satan would've given Him a *supposed* kingdom.

However, Satan had no power to bend Jesus over to such a heinous transaction. Because Jesus took the time to fast, pray, and fuel on the Word of God, He was aware of the temptations that awaited Him. So, He fought back with the Word of God, "It is written, Man shall not live by bread alone, but by every word that proceeds from the mouth of God" Matthew 4:4.

Our Lord knew the importance of living off God's daily bread – the Word of God. Jesus knew that should He have the strength to endure all that awaited Him; He needed the Word in His system.

Therefore, as a result of daily fasting, praying, and meditating on the Word of God, Jesus was able to resist the devil. Likewise, the same is required of us. Within the Lord's prayer, God designated a segment just for asking for His Daily Bread. Having the Word of God within your system is not only to remember and recite scriptures but mainly to know God's heart and to use His Word as an armor against the evil one. Now, more than ever, we need the Word of God.

Yet, it's simply not enough to know Scriptures. We must live by scriptures and become engulfed in the Word of God to the point that His glory and His nature permeate through us.

Moreover, walking and living in God's glory can only come from a sincere desire to feed on His Daily Bread – God's Word. Therefore, we must desire and ask for His Word to illuminate through us.

As we pray, "give us this day our daily bread," by faith, we must believe that God is a rewarder of those who diligently seek Him Hebrews 11:6. We must believe that, should we seek His face, search the scriptures and meditate on His Word, then we will be sustained by His Word.

*And forgive us our debts...*

The beautiful thing about fueling on God's Word is that you understand the importance of repentance. After you've gone into your secret place and acknowledged the Lord, gave praises to Him, asked of His purpose, and desired more of Him, now is the right time to ask for forgiveness. It's essential that before asking for a request from God, you ask for forgiveness of sins as well as forgive others of their faults against you.

Not asking for forgiveness is almost like having an argument with an individual only to have them ask for a favor without apologizing, or coming to terms of agreement with the wrong that was done. You'll feel awful about this, and if you carry out the request, you'll grudgingly do so. Not coming to terms after an agreement

*Prayer Tool*

leaves legal access for the enemy to come into your life and sow seeds of contention and discord.

No wonder, Matthew 6:12 says to continue in prayer, by submitting such a request unto the Lord, as it states, "And forgive us our debts, as we forgive our debtors" To God, unforgiveness equates to committing sin.

Also, the dictionary definition of debt is sin. We should ensure to repent and forgive others before asking for any request from the Father. Holding onto sins and grudges can block many blessings, burn unnecessary bridges, and cause you to abort a mission that has or has yet to begin.

### *And do not lead us into temptation...*

"And lead us not into temptation, but deliver us from the evil one. For Yours is the kingdom and the power and the glory forever. Amen." Matthew 6:13 works in two-folds, it's a desire to continue in the Lord's path. But if we consider closely, we'll see that it's also a request that's followed by praise. Therefore, what is your request? What do you desire from God? What are your needs?

You've been faithful about seeking the Lord, you've honored Him, and you're even "working out your own salvation with fear and trembling" Philippians 2:12. Now is the time to ask, and make your request known to Him. Though, when you ask, you must do so by faith. Believe that whatever you asked for, by faith, you'll receive.

And lastly, just as Mathew 6:13 ended with praise, 'Yours is the kingdom and the power and the glory forever,' ensure that praise continues in your heart. Remember to praise God in all situations, for He is worthy to be praised.

In John 15:7, Jesus tells us that if we abide in Him and His Words are in us, then if we ask of anything in His name, it will be done. Take note of the factors that have taken place prior to Jesus' stating that 'it will be done.' He says if we abide in Him, and His Words in us, then whatever we ask, we'll receive. The outline of the Lord's prayer is the definition of abiding in Him and He in You.

God gives us an overview of prayer as a guide and format. Your prayer life should be one that is unique to the Father while implementing His desires. Without considering the Heart of Christ, your prayers will become self-centered.

Should you desire to see a breakthrough in your life, your family, this world, and see His Kingdome come? Then I encourage you to practice incorporating God's model prayer.

## *Prayer Tool*

*Sample, yet powerful prayers that you can incorporate daily.*

Father, You're worthy, Lord, I adore You. You are the creator of all of Heaven and earth, and I thank You. Father, I thank You for all that You've done in my life and the lives of my Family. Lord, I ask that You forgive me for all that I've done that has caused a separation between us. Father, I also ask that You reveal anything hidden in my heart that is not of You. Father, continue to establish Your love in my life and keep me in Your path. In Jesus' name, I pray, amen.

Dear Heavenly Father, Lord, I thank You. Father, I bless Your name. Lord, I ask that You continue to come into my life and purify my heart. Father, I ask that if there is anything in me that is not of You, Lord, in Jesus' name, remove it. Father, I desire to be more like You. So, Father, continue to establish me in Your image. In Your Son, Jesus' name, I pray, amen.

## Chapter | 2

## Heart Posture

### The Spirit of Forgiveness

Matthew 6:14 speaks volumes. When you keep your eyes and ears open to what the Spirit of the Lord has to say concerning forgiveness and prayer, then you'll be ushered into a wealth of breakthroughs. It's amazing that right after the Lord's prayer, Jesus proceeds by stating, "For if you forgive men their trespasses, your heavenly Father will also forgive you. But if you do not forgive men their trespasses, neither will your Father forgive your trespasses".

*Prayer Tool*

Even further, Mark 11:25 Tells us that if we're holding anything against anyone while entering into prayer, we should forgive them so that God may forgive us. Likewise, Matthew 5:24 warns us to first leave our gifts, worship, and offerings at the altar (and not present it to God) before reconciling with our brother. Once reconciliation has taken place, then we should proceed to offer our gifts and worship to God.

There are simply some prayers that'll never be answered when we allow unforgiveness to fester in our hearts. God is a good Father, and He wants nothing more than to lavish blessings on His children, "according to His riches in glory by Christ Jesus" Philippians 4:19.

However, because "rebellion is as the sin of witchcraft" 1 Samuel 15:23, many are blocking their blessings. Therefore, we must purify our souls and be reconciled with our brothers so that we can adequately posture our hearts before the Lord.

Thankfully, purification begins the moment you acknowledge and repent. Romans 10:10 tells us that "with the heart, one believes unto righteousness, and with the mouth, confession is made unto salvation." Isn't that incredible?

While this scripture deals with the sanctification process and being born again through Christ Jesus, the same still applies to prayer. "Because out of the abundance of the heart, the mouth speaks" Luke 6:45. Hence, we must acknowledge and confess our faults to God. And when we acknowledge our faults, we should be truthful and sincere. No shades, no sheets, no covering — before the God who sees everything.

Assessing our hearts must be a daily habit. As we find anything that is not of God, we ought to take it to the Lord, ask Him to forgive us, and allow Him to show us the way we should go.

Nevertheless, repenting has to mean that you intend to turn away from whatever separated you from God. And you're not intentionally committing the same action, repeatedly. Instead, you're choosing to walk in the precepts of the Lord.

For example, if someone hits you and says that they're sorry, their efforts will validate their words. If this same individual intentionally hits you again, chances are, you'll find it hard to believe the sincerity of their apology. Because repentance confirms what the mouth speaks, the inclination toward repentance and forgiveness must be established in the heart.

*Preparation of the heart*

A heart posture that is established in the Lord has a foundation in God. Quite often, when the Lord wants you to address an area within your soul, He'll bring it to the forefront of your mind. God does this to soften and prepare your heart. The Lord prepares your heart to either receive an individual or to make amends with someone.

*Prayer Tool*

Just like one day, as I was driving, the Lord dropped a name into my spirit and told me they'd be calling soon. Little did I know they would call two days later. I genuinely believe that if the Lord never spoke into my heart, I would've been reluctant to speak with this person. Nevertheless, the Lord prepared me, and I was able to receive the grace that followed our conversation.

Even so, as the Lord prepares your heart to either receive an individual or forgive someone, whether you can express it to them or not, allow the process to soften your heart.

The process of pruning and softening your heart will often involve humility and honesty. Can you humble yourself enough to admit that you may have been at fault? Are you bold enough to confess that you've been hurt? Are you strong enough to walk into forgiveness? If you are, then be prepared to be immersed in God's grace. God is infatuated with a heart that knows how to forgive and forgive gracefully.

God delights in the spirit of forgiveness because He has forgiven us much. Moreover, we're made in His image. Therefore, forgiveness is engraved in our DNA; however, unforgiveness is not. Unforgiveness is a learned behavior that stems from hurt, shame, pride, and insecurity. Unforgiveness is not of God; therefore, we must rid our hearts of such before prayer.

## *The Highest Command – LOVE*

The perfect remedy for unforgiveness is love. And the perfect ingredient to add in prayer is love. You can pray an entire house down, but if you lack love, then it's all for nothing. You can have eloquent speech and a diverse vernacular, but the lack of love will cause you to sound like a clanging cymbal. In all things, you need love to thrive.

As believers of Jesus Christ, we're called ambassadors and co-heirs of the Kingdom of Heaven. As we take on our royal partnership with Jesus, we must be mindful of the state of our hearts.

Yet, we can't take inventory of our faults all by ourselves. We need the Lord. In Jeremiah 17:9, the Lord asks if there's anyone who truly knows the heart because it is deceitful and wicked. God knows that the heart is driven by our emotions, feelings, and desires. As a result, if we follow the leading of our heart or try to clarify our emotions, we'll be led astray till we're left to wander off in the schemes of our minds, versus the Lord's.

Luckily, the Lord answered Jeremiah's question in the proceeding verse when He said, "I, the Lord, search the heart, I test the mind, even to give every man according to his ways, according to the fruit of his doings" Jeremiah 17:10.

Should we mature in prayer, we must take account of the state of our heart by asking the Lord to reveal it.

## In Christ, Jesus

To establish a prayer-ready heart posture, we must be in the Lord. We must desire His presence. Most importantly, we can be sure that God desires to be in our presence. In John 15:5 & 9-11, Jesus tells us to abide in Him as He abides in us. He abides in us because He loves us with the Father's heart.

In addition, the Father also states that following in His precepts is how we express our love towards Him. Therefore, as God is love, we must remain in Christ Jesus so that we, too, can share in His love.

One of many attributes of God is that He is a loving and relational Father. He is a God who cares about His creation. He is a Father who seeks after His sons and daughters. He is a Creator who desires to know His creation.

And what better way to live than spending our entire lives searching and getting to know our Father? Building a relationship with God is inevitable. So, why not seek the Father while He can be found?

Though, I think it's vital to express the simplicity of seeking Jesus. I believe many find it hard to build a relationship with Christ due to thoughts of its complexity. Christ tells us to take up our cross and follow Him.

To follow Christ is to submit to Him and seek His ways daily. Surely, this includes praying, fasting, reading His Word, etc. Most Importantly, these practices enhance your relationship with the Father.

A time may come when our church accessibility and our Bibles become sparse, as such is the case now. So, what do you do? Suppose you never step foot in a church again nor crack open the Bible? Do you still seek ways to know the Lord? Do you practice sitting at His feet just for the sake? Or do you get entangled in the seemingly prevailing situation?

There's a story in the Bible where Jesus paid two sisters, Mary and Martha, a visit. Martha was serving as she saw fit to wait on Jesus and serve. However, on the other hand, Mary chose not to serve.

As a result, Martha questioned Jesus and figured He should've chastised Mary for not helping her out. Instead, Jesus was well pleased with Mary as she found quietly sitting at the feet of Jesus was more valuable. Mary knew the importance of resting in the presence of the Lord, and that pleased Jesus.

There's value in the simplicity of resting at the feet of Jesus. Though all the customs of honoring and worshiping Christ are perfectly fine, we must take heed, that should all else fail, we never cease from knowing the Lord, in Spirit and in truth.

## *Prayer Tool*

### *Personal Prayer*

Having the heart of Jesus and knowing who He is, is mandatory for an effective prayer life. If one overlooks the necessity of living a life of love, honor, and repentance, the chances of getting consumed in your flesh are high. We must come into prayer from a personal relationship stance.

You can reflect and ask these questions: who is the Father to you? Do you know the Lord? Do you desire to know God? We shouldn't come to the Father only because we have a need and feel as if a quick prayer is the solution. It's insulting. You should desire the Lord and rest at His feet simply because He is Lord, and you love Him.

However, everyone's walk with Christ is different. Therefore, you mustn't be comparing your walk with someone else's. Most importantly, receive the grace needed for your own walk, and walk therein.

Whether you are a seasoned believer or a newborn Christian, know that your walk with the Lord is ever-changing. Personally, earlier in my walk with Christ, I read the Word of God night and day. I desired His Word, I wanted to know who He is, so I sought after Him. Even so, as I'm maturing, I now know the Word of God. Therefore, I meditate on it. I remind myself of the scriptures.

Because I spent much time being engulfed in His Word and presence, I am now consumed with His Spirit; He resides in my soul.

Though I still read the Bible, my quiet time with Jesus seem much different compared to when I was a babe in Christ.

And yes, the same is true for you. We're called to go from glory to glory and from faith to faith. We are continually growing, maturing, and forming into the image of Christ. Our evolution in Jesus can only come from truly knowing the King – the Lord our God. But you must first desire it.

God is a Gentleman, and He gives His children the option of 'choice.' You can choose to forgive. You can choose to repent. You can choose to love. And if you want to, you can choose to desire the presence of the Lord. However, I stand with Jesus, and I want to encourage you to choose life Deuteronomy 30:15-20.

## *Prayer Tool*

The intention of 'Heart Posture' is to focus on the matter of your heart. As you draw closer to Jesus and continue to grow in prayer, continue to take inventory.

However, an accurate account can only come from the Spirit of the Lord. Therefore, our Prayer Tool is focused on God leading your Heart Posture as you continue to grow and mature.

**Dear Abba,**

Lord, You are glorious. Father, You are God. You are the King of kings and Lord of lords. Father, I love and adore You. Lord, there is none like You. Oh, Father, You search the earth looking for someone who will honor You in spirit and truth. Oh my God, You desire a people who are after Your heart.

Abba, search my heart, test my mind, and establish me in Your precepts. Establish me in Your will. Father, I desire to have a Heart Posture that is in alignment with You. Lord mold me in Your image.

Oh, Father, how marvelous are Your works. Lord, You created the Heavens and the Earth and how glorious are Your works! Lord, I know You will do a great work in me. So, Father, build me, prune and establish me, my sweet King. In Your only Begotten Son Jesus' Name, I pray. I love You, Father. Amen.

## Chapter | 3

## Spirit of Worship

Worship. It's so much more than praising, singing, and dancing during the first thirty minutes of service. Worship is an outward expression of your inward faith. Worship is a deep level of intimacy that connects you to the Father. Worship is a lifestyle.

Worship is a war cry. Worship is a weapon of warfare. Worship is honoring God through your obedience. Worship, when in spirit and in truth, pleases the Father.

## The Mechanism of our Heart

Just like God is three in one, the Father, Son, and the Holy Spirit, we too are triune beings. We have our physical body that is visibly seen. Then we have our soul that's comprised of all earthly matters such as our emotions and thoughts. Lastly and most importantly, we have our spirit, which connects us to the Father.

Our spirit consists of everything that pertains to the Kingdom of Heaven. Jointly, our soul and spirit are what breeds life. Our soul contains our earthly life, and our spirit is what we'll manifest in life eternally. When it comes to our body, it's the shell or moving mechanism that's driven and controlled by both our soul and spirit.

Our entire body is under the submission of the Spirit. Still, all organs, such as our hearts and mind, are within the providence of our soul. When it comes to our hearts, it's in constant communication with our brain. As our mind receives, our heart perceives, and likewise, as our heart receives, our mind perceives.

Because of this, we have scripture that tells us that with our hearts, we believe, *and* as we think, so are we. Furthermore, everything that's physically done is in constant and joint control of our hearts and mind.

God knows that we are spirit-filled beings that are often motivated by our emotions or, in other words, our soul/flesh. Therefore, we have the wisdom of Luke 6:45, which informs us that as we speak, we utter the contents of our hearts.

*Out of your heart*

Worship is another form of prayer. It's a physical act that is spiritual and allows us to connect and communicate with the Father. When we worship, we're pouring out the contents of our heart – our soul, that's why we're cautioned in Proverbs 4:23 to guard our hearts because our issues of life spring forth.

To guard our hearts is to protect the sanctity of our soul and spirit. It means, feeding on the Word of God versus soaking in the cares of this world. Guarding the heart entails meditating on God's thoughts towards us and not people's labels on our lives.

As we guard our hearts, we're getting our minds consumed with scriptural things and allowing Jesus to conform us to His image. As we're shaped and conformed in His image, our worship will reflect it.

If you're one who hardly seeks God, and is consumed with worldly things, then your worship will reveal it. Your worship will either be nonexistent or consist of distractions, awkwardness, or uncertainty. When you're consumed with anything other than the goodness of Jesus, it'll be evident. Worship symbolizes an outward expression of your inward faith.

Likewise, when you fuel on the goodness of Jesus, rest at His feet and earnestly desire His presence, then your worship will reveal your heart for God.

Then, you begin to understand that God is so good and ought to be praised. Your worship is never contingent on a program; neither does it rest on what your neighbor is doing. Instead, your worship is a reflection of your thoughts towards Jesus and your desire to honor Him.

### *Lifestyle of Worship*

As a child of God, you need to understand that in all circumstances, worship is needed. Therefore, your worship is never isolated based on your needs, neither can it be quenched nor ignited through your feelings. As someone who's heart is vested in Jesus, your worship has to become your lifestyle.

We're called ambassadors of Christ. We are Christ's earthly agents and representatives. We're called to be Jesus' hands and feet and to operate as He would.

Most importantly, though we're in this world, we must remain set apart as we're co-heirs to the Kingdom. Therefore, we must walk with the fragrant of Heaven and honor God with a lifestyle of worship. To honor God with a lifestyle of worship is considering Christ in all our ways. We seek to know the mind of Jesus when we walk in His wisdom. And we become one with Him through an understanding of His will.

Because we're in a constant lifestyle of worship, we know the importance of worshipping and loving God always. The same applies to knowing how to be abased and knowing how to abound Philippians 4:12.

We understand that godliness with contentment is great gain 1 Timothy 6:6. Therefore, we're not rattled by our circumstances. Instead, we submit all our issues to the Father and rest. And as we rest, we surrender to the will of God, knowing that His desires are chief among all others.

Living a lifestyle of worship does not mean that everything will always be lilies and roses. Therefore, with all your heart, your trust must remain in the Lord. You must consciously choose to not lean on your own understanding, so that you could acknowledge God in all your ways, knowing that He'll direct your path Provers 3:5-6. A lifestyle of worship is surrendering your soul/flesh to the Father and entrusting Him with your spirit.

## Obedience in Worship

We're all familiar with the infamous story of the city of Jericho. We know how the children of Israel marched around the walls and won their battle. However, before the children of Israel could obtain victory, they first needed obedience in worship.

This is why I believe, as you engage in worship, the Spirit of God will examine the posture of your heart. God wants to ensure that your heart is pliable towards Him. He needs to know that you're not going through the motions of worship, but instead, you desire to reverence Him. God needs to know your heart posture because He wishes to use you for His Glory.

Joshua, in chapter 3, began the journey to take the children of Israel to the Promised Land. In their journey, they had numerous instructions, which was only revealed after the prior had been accomplished. They were the epitome of walking by faith and not by sight. In fact, Israel had to wait on the Lord for their next step. They were heading towards uncharted territory since they have never been to where the Lord was taking them.

Therefore, their first direction was to follow the Ark of the Covenant. Following the Ark of the covenant meant obedience through worship, as the Ark was an emblem of the glory of the Lord.

Often, when the Lord is taking you into a new journey and a new phase in life, He will use your weapon of worship, to get you there. Your obedience in worship is vital because though you may have a glimpse of your destination, chances are, you may be unsure of the process.

Also, as we pour out our worship to the Lord, we are ridding ourselves of everything that is not of God and fueling on His goodness. Thus, creating a foundation and preparing ourselves for God.

Therefore, the foundation of worship is to build our faith, understanding, and trust in our Father. As our faith becomes established, we'll begin to grow from faith to faith and from glory to glory.

### *His Spirit goes before you*

As the children of Israel honored and followed the Lord, they were then instructed in verse 5 of chapter 3, to sanctify themselves for the Lord was ready to perform wonders before them. It's important to note that before miracles, they were to sanctify themselves. Sanctification prepared their hearts and minds to receive the manifestation of God's glory. Too often are people missing out on the splendors of the Lord, simply because they refuse to get sanctified.

Sanctification is when one purifies their heart and soul to the Lord. As you sanctify yourself, you're allowing the Holy Spirit to wash you clean through the Word of God and the renewing of your mind.

Sanctification is a spiritual cleansing of the temple within our Heart. To become sanctified, we must immerse ourselves in the presence of the Lord. We must allow the Holy Spirit to purge us of anything that is not of Him, and then fill us up with His Spirit.

The children of Israel had the promise of obtaining the city of Jericho, yet the Jordan River separated them. I believe that if the children of Israel never sanctified themselves, they may never have been ready for what was going to take place. Chances are they could have been filled with doubt and fear. They could've looked at the Jordan as a deterrent and refused to believe God. Yet, because they sanctified themselves, their hearts were receptive to the move of God, and the Lord was able to perform His Word.

We must remain in constant communication with the Father. Such a connection is needed for our lives. Since the children of Israel honored the Lord through worship and obedience, they were then able to hear from God. Also, their hearts and minds were not troubled because they were sanctified by the time they encountered the Jordan River. Therefore, the Lord was able to move before them to part and dry the Jordan.

Often, the Lord will use your level of obedience to test and build your faith. As your faith is established, the Lord can then trust you with His glory and the fruition of His Word. The Lord needs to know that you're a willing and able vessel that He can use and trust. He desires to remove your barriers, but He must ensure that your faith is sturdy and that your belief can carry you even when it appears as if God's promises won't come to pass.

As the Lord moves miraculously, we must keep in mind that the glory is all for Him. Notice that the entire chapter of Joshua 4 is devoted to the fact that God delivered the children of Israel through the Jordan because He is God.

Therefore, as the Lord increases you, ensure that you're keeping Him at the forefront of your elevation. Remember that all glory belongs to Him. Therefore, we must remain in constant worship to remind ourselves of what the Father has done for us, knowing that it's neither due to our strength nor our means.

## Dawn of a New Day

Joshua, chapter 4, ended with the children of Israel preparing for battle. For them, it was the Dawn of a New Day. Though the Lord had performed miracles, what they were about to witness was unheard of. Therefore, in preparation, they were to become circumcised — a representation of baptism. Also, the

Commander of the Lord's army (who I believe was Jesus) visited Joshua as a sign that God was fighting for them.

**Worship is a powerful weapon of Warfare**

I believe, if the Lord were to tell us the complete process by which His will would be done, chances are, we may not follow through. The Lord knows that not every step and phase in our journey will be favorable and comfortable. Therefore, He does not reveal the entire picture to the puzzle, only the pieces we need to see. Likewise, the same is true for the children of Israel. The Lord simply told them that they were to conquer Jericho. However, He didn't reveal all they would encounter, neither did He allude to the fact that it was going to be easy to access.

As the children of Israel approached the doors of Jericho, they found they were completely shut. There were no entry points that would make their accessibility seamless. As a people who followed the Lord and was obedient to fulfill all that He instructed, it would appear as if the final mile would be smooth sailing. However, they were stuck at the gates, needing divine intervention. So, they rested in worship and relied on the Lord.

Often, our real test comes from not only obeying the Lord but trusting Him amid what seems impossible. Ephesians 6:13 tells us to stand after we've put on the whole armor of God. After we've done everything the Lord instructed us to do, with no stones left unturned, we must stand and wait. Fortunately, that was what the children of Israel did.

Shortly after, the Lord gave them instructions. The elders were to blow their horns as the children of Israel silently walked around the walls of Jericho. They were to repeat this cycle of blowing and silently marching once per day, for six days. Marching quietly was imperative.

Though we participate in the battle, there is spiritual warfare in the spiritual realm, hidden away from our physical senses. As a result, we must move obediently, as the Lord leads. If the children of Israel made any sound, chances are Jericho's gates would not have fallen as they did.

**Worship opens Heaven's Gates**

After perpetually honoring God through obedience and worship, the children of Israel had a breakthrough. On the seventh day, the children were directed to shout during an appointed time. As they shouted, the walls of Jericho fell.

In addition to a sweet victory, they took some of the goods of the land. Only a few designated treasures were brought into the treasury of the Lord.

As you are being pruned, groomed, and matured in the spirit of worship, remain steadfast and obedient. Just as the example of the children of Israel, the Lord will take you through numerous trails during your faith walk.

As the Lord takes you through diverse phases of life, the Lord will monitor your heart of worship. He'll like to know if you will worship Him in spirit and in truth, even through known and unknown variables.

Through the good and the tough times, what would be the posture of your heart? The Lord is looking for willing and able vessels whom He can use and take from glory to glory for His Kingdom.

*It's in your Spirit*

Even though worship appears as a physical act, yet, it must originate within our spirit. In essence, our worship should be in spirit and in truth. John 4:24 tells us that 'God is Spirit, and those who worship Him must worship in spirit and truth.'

To worship God means that our entire being is in alignment. Our heart posture, our thought process, and our desires are all aligned with the intentions of honoring and reverencing God.

God is Spirit; therefore, we must understand that God is aware of the content of our hearts. Yet, many are holding on to themselves. When we come before God in prayer, we must acknowledge that He is omnipresent, and He cares about every aspect of our lives.

Therefore, we must let go of all inhibitions. We must submit all negative thoughts, all preconceived notions, and all fleshly desires under the authority and obedience of Jesus Christ. We must come into the full knowledge of who God is and what He is capable of.

God is pure and holy in all His ways. Therefore, He requires the same from us. However, this does not mean that we're perfect in our own ways. Instead, this means that we're perfect in God.

Finally, remember that all have sinned and fallen short of the glory of God. So, when you worship, you must acknowledge your imperfection. You must admit that you are sinful in your flesh, but God is holy. Yet, in the holiness of divine nature, God still desires to meet with you. God still loves you; He always wants to clean you up, and He still desires to commune with you.

Indeed, God desires your worship.

## Prayer Tool
*Prayers of Worship*

**Praise the Lord!**

"Sing to the Lord a new song, and His praise in the assembly of saints. Let Israel rejoice in their Maker; Let the children of Zion be joyful in their King. Let them praise His name with the dance; Let them sing praises to Him with the timbrel and harp for the Lord takes pleasure in His people; He will beautify the humble with salvation. Let the saints be joyful in glory; Let them sing aloud on their beds. Let the high praises of God be in their mouth." Amen Psalm 149:1-6.

**Praise the Lord!**

"Praise God in His sanctuary; praise Him in His mighty firmament! Praise Him for His mighty acts; Praise Him according to His excellent greatness! Praise Him with the sound of the trumpet; Praise Him with the lute and harp! Praise Him with the timbrel and dance; Praise Him with stringed instruments and flutes! Praise Him with loud cymbals; Praise Him with clashing cymbals! Let everything that has breath praise the Lord. Praise the Lord!" Amen. Psalm 15

## Chapter | 4

## Tongues of Worship

When worship becomes a lifestyle, it breaks barriers. Worship opens doors that your natural mind could never fathom. It disengages your thoughts, emotions, and human understanding while inclining your ears to Heaven. With an ear inclined to the voice of the Lord, you can receive divine information and wisdom on how to fight your battles, as most battles can only be won through worship.

Moreover, worship is mandatory, as most individuals are not privy to the fact that they're in spiritual warfare. Therefore, God gave us the gift of tongues, which — besides being a higher form of interaction with God — is our spiritual weapon and our tool in both prayer and worship.

The gift of speaking in tongues is available to all who believe in Jesus Christ. But to receive the gift of speaking in tongues, one must desire it and believe by faith that they've received it. And after they desire and believe in the gift of speaking in tongues, they must activate their spiritual language and put it to use, by faith. This is because, just like anything that is newly learned, the gift of tongues is not always fully developed or pronounced at first.

Therefore, just as you practiced walking and talking, you must actively press into the Holy Spirit, and by faith, speak as He gives you utterance. Then, you'll be able to gradually articulate your spiritual language.

### *Rivers of Never-ending Water*

I want to share with you how I received the gift of speaking in tongues. It was at an amazing conference I attended just within a few months of rededicating my life back to Christ. At this event, the atmosphere was thick with the presence of the Lord: signs, wonders, and deliverances were happening everywhere.

So, during the first night of the conference, everyone who hadn't spoken in tongues was encouraged to stir up their gift and speak as the Lord moved. At that time, I remember having a desperate desire to speak in tongues, so I prayed, earnestly asking the Lord for my gift. Then I spoke something out by faith. I was amazed that I spoke in tongues, but I was also confused.

I wondered why my tongues only sounded like a soft rolling 'rr' sound. While everyone else around me sounded like *'Ra-sha-tah-da-da'* with so much force and confidence. Yet, I kept practicing and speaking in tongues

However, throughout that entire three-day conference, that first night was the only night I spoke in tongues. And it wasn't because I couldn't; I was embarrassed. I felt as if I was doing it wrong, and perhaps I didn't speak in tongues as I thought. And during my ride home, my confusion continued. So, I took to Google to see if there was such a thing as 'false tongues' and tried to figure out if tongues were something of God or not.

Let's just say the enemy had a field day with my mind. After my seven-hour ride, I concluded that I had not spoken in tongues, and in fact, it was something of the devil and not of the Lord. As a result, I settled with thinking that if it was the Lord, He would make my mouth move, and I would feel this grand emotion and sensation as proof that the Holy Spirit was with me.

After that, years went by without me having this ecstatic experience I sought, and I hadn't spoken in tongues again. So, I wondered if I was doing something wrong. Wasn't I trying hard enough? Wasn't I praying long enough? I couldn't understand it.

*Prayer Tool*

I was well into leading Rise Ministry and began questioning why God didn't do it for me. I tried, I prayed, I fasted, I had my prayer partner pray with me and over me so that I can speak in tongues. Even my mom prayed for me. But nothing worked, so I continued to settle with the notion that God will do it for me when *He's* ready.

Although I didn't speak in tongues, years later, I still raved about that conference. It was and still is an amazing and life-changing experience. Even more so, I encouraged my mentee to go. I knew it would be life-changing and would draw her closer to Christ.

Well, after her experience, she called me to tell me all the great news and the impact it had on her. Then, she dropped the bomb, '*And Mani, guess WHAT??... I spoke in tongues!*" I could've yelled if I hadn't been on the phone with her.

I was genuinely excited, and I rejoiced with her, but I had a bone to pick with God. After my conversation with her, I began to press God. I couldn't understand how my mentee spoke in tongues before me. *I mean, God! Come on, I'm mentoring her. Why hadn't I spoke in tongues yet?* However, during my questioning, God answered me; He said that I had to repent and press into the Holy Spirit.

Therefore, a day after I spoke with my friend, I hit my prayer room. I repented for assuming that I hadn't spoken in tongues and apologized for thinking it was God's responsibility to *make my mouth move*.

In prayer, I came to understand that God is a gentle Father and will not make us do anything against our will. After all, He allowed us to choose Him and gives us the ability to speak in tongues if we want. So, once I had repented, I understood that the ball was in my court. I played worship music, blessed the Lord, and thanked Him for giving me the gift of tongues.

Because of my experience, I wanted an example. You wouldn't believe what I did. As I was worshipping, I thought about the way my mom's tongues sounded. By faith, I started moving my mouth and imitated the sounds of my mother. Well, after an hour of futility, I was so tired that I prayed out.

The next day was time for round two. I put on my spiritual boxing gloves, rebuked the devil, commanded that my spirit aligned with the Fathers', and declared that I spoke in tongues. Round two was a shift for me.

After about twenty-to-thirty minutes of worshipping, the Holy Spirit filled my room, and I spoke in tongues powerfully. I couldn't stop it!. And as I spoke, John 7:38 came alive within me. Out of my heart flowed rivers of living water.

That day was emotional for me. I could not believe that I spoke in tongues and with authoritative utterances to match. And NO, I did not sound like my mom. I had my own, divinely inspired spiritual language. It was amazing!

After my worship session, the Holy Spirit explained why my tongues were so powerful. He told me that my experience many years ago was authentic. I was told that my soft rolling 'rr' sound, were tongues and simply needed maturing. And because the gift was dormant, when I opened my mouth again, it was like a backed-up fire hydrant that was released. Rivers of never-ending water flowed from my spirit.

The gift of tongues is a powerful tool and isn't for a selected few. In fact, all believers of Jesus Christ have access to speaking in tongues. However, you must believe.

The truth is, the devil hates the gift of speaking in tongues. He can't understand it, nor can he imitate God's gift. But the enemy knows that if the body of Christ truly understands the power of speaking in tongues, then the kingdom of darkness will be defeated. So he tries to frustrate our experience with doubt, fear, and confusion concerning this incredible gift.

You must keep this in mind. Satan, the deceiver, does not want you to unlock your heavenly language. Speaking in tongues is a gift from God and is Heaven's language on earth.

### *Heaven's Language*

Though speaking in tongues is predominantly a heavenly language in which our spirit communicates with the Spirit of God, the gift of speaking in tongues also impacts us. The gift of tongues reveals

Heavenly secrets concerning you and as well as others. It brings forth healing, draws you closer to Christ, and wages war in the spiritual.

The gift of speaking in tongues is a powerful tool and should be utilized more, within our churches and in our personal lives. Indeed, if we press into God's presence through spiritual worship and engage with Heaven's gift, then we're bound to see a rebirth of the acts of God.

## Tongues of Fire

Once Jesus ascended into Heaven, He sent the Holy Spirit to empower His disciples for the Great Commission. And much like today, Jesus' Spirit, the Holy Spirit was to guide and lead them in the path in which they should go. Also, the day the Holy Spirit was sent to the earth in Acts chapter 2, all who were assembled spoke in a Heavenly language. The gift of speaking in tongues was a sign that His Holy Spirit was with them.

After the disciples were endowed with the gift of speaking in tongues, their next assignment was revealed. Through the impressions and interpretations of tongues, the disciples knew that they were to gather men and place them in leadership within the provisions of God.

We must understand that God cares about our every need. However, our human senses limit spiritual revelation. Therefore, all things are revealed to us through the Spirit of God. Our gift of speaking in tongues reveals the motives and intentions that God has for us.

Just as the disciples received divine information from speaking in tongues, those who weren't assembled nor received the gift, received Heavenly insight as well.

Moreover, when the Holy Spirit released tongues of fire on the day of Pentecost, bystanders heard of the wonders of God. In Acts 2:7-8, we see that the crowd was amazed at what they heard. Each one testified that they heard what was being said in their native language. Obviously, God reveals His glory and the mysteries of Heaven through the gift of speaking in tongues.

We must eagerly speak in tongues as our heavenly language is not only for us but also a sign for the unbeliever 1 Corinthians 14:22. Because as we speak in tongues, much like the days of Acts, God's glory transcends beyond us, revealing the love of Christ to all who are present. When we utter our heavenly language, we are actively partnering with Heaven to draw unbelievers closer to Christ.

### *Mysteries of Heaven*

When we pray in tongues, the Bible tells us that we communicate divine secrets that we are unaware of. The Holy Spirit intercedes for us according to the will of God.

We know from Romans 8:26-27 that the Holy Spirit helps us when we're weak. When we don't contain the language or understanding of what's happening around us or within us - the Holy Spirit is well informed.

Indeed, there are times you might have a burden to pray, yet you don't know what to pray for. In such times, the gifts of speaking in tongues are vital. The Holy Spirit dwells within the human spirit, and He directs us on what to do and how to pray.

One evening, during my ride home, I intended to pray in tongues until I reached home. But the Lord cautioned me not to quench the Holy Spirit. Therefore, after I arrived home, I remained in my car and continued to pray. Immediately after praying in the Holy Spirit, I felt a shift in my body. Unexplainable healing took place. I had no idea that I needed healing. However, my spirit did. And because of my obedience to praying, the Lord healed me in places I never knew needed healing.

Indeed, God wishes to have His way in our lives, but we must yield to Him. Furthermore, as we yield to the Holy Spirit, He reveals areas of our lives that need tending to and brings them under Christ's authority. Yes, healings and miracles occur under and by the authority of Jesus. John 11 shares the story of how Lazarus was raised from the dead.

When Lazarus died, his sisters, Martha and Mary, called for Jesus. They knew that Jesus could heal and, therefore, expected Him to restore their brother's life. However, when they sent for Jesus, He delayed and chose to visit Lazarus in His own time. You see, Jesus understood that He had authority that transcended the boundaries of time. Therefore, He was neither anxious nor in haste.

Jesus waited two days before tending to the needs of His friend. Once Jesus arrived at Lazarus' gravesite, Martha hurried to His side. She blamed Him for His tardiness, stating that if He'd come sooner, her brother would be alive.

But, Jesus declared that Lazarus would live again. Yet, Martha, being skeptical and fearful, ran into the comfort of her sister and the rest of the community. As Martha and Mary looked to the city for consolidation, they forgot what Jesus said.

We must remember the promises of the Lord. If we're not careful, we could become like Martha and Mary; take matters in our own hands and rush in front of God. Or, just as they, we can have an unsettled spirit and run to our community looking for validation.

Nonetheless, when God promises, He is faithful to see it through. And although Jesus heard the doubt in Martha and Mary, He prayed. The Word of God said that Jesus groaned in His Spirit twice and gave thanks to God for hearing His prayer. Afterward, He belted out. "Lazarus, come forth." At the sound of Jesus' voice, Lazarus resurrected.

Jesus is all-powerful and understands the power of praying in the Spirit. Because everyone around Jesus doubted, He knew that His groans and praying in the Spirit would bind those seeds of doubt and release His power of life.

Think about it. If Jesus, who is God in the flesh, utilized the power of praying in the Spirit, then how much more should we? Admittedly, we must align our hearts in the posture of faith and believe that just as Jesus prayed and moved mountains, as we pray in tongues, the mountains will also move.

**Wrapped in His arms**

James 4:8 tells us to draw near to God, and He will draw near to us. Speaking in tongues is Heaven's prayer language that brings us closer to the Father. As we pray in the Spirit, our spirit connects with the Holy Spirit, creating a deeper level of intimacy.

In line with this, as people having deep fellowship with the Father, we ought not to conform to the world. Instead, we're to be separate and conform to the image of Christ.

Also, because speaking in tongues immerses us into the presence of the Lord, our flesh must come under His authority. And once our flesh surrenders to Jesus, everything that is not of God is revealed and dealt with.

Now, we all know that the Bible calls the enemy *the accuser*. This is because the enemy watches God's children with intentions of creating a stumbling block. The devil knows that God's intentions are for men to honor Jesus and to live a life that pleases Him. Therefore, Satan looks for faults and flaws so that he can antagonize the people of God.

Satan's accusations are what produces shame and condemnation, thus separating us from God. However, God knows that all have sinned and fallen short of His glory Romans 3:23. Therefore, God gave us His Holy Spirit to comfort and direct us.

Nonetheless, as we willingly draw closer to God, we begin to conform more to His image. In the process, we are reducing the amount of demonic accusations. After all, how can Satan accuse you, if you don't give him anything to work with?

But, reduced accusations does not mean that Satan won't try to accuse you. Instead, because you're intentional about sitting at the Father's feet, Satan's accusations will not stick. You've become transformed into the beauty of Jesus.

Now, although the amount of accusations may decrease, that does not mean attacks and spiritual warfare will. It's important to understand that being a child of God does not exempt you from spiritual warfare nor struggles.

Instead, being a child of God means that through the Holy Spirit, you have the tools that are needed to sustain you as you wage a good warfare and fight the good fight of faith.

## *Sword of the Spirit*

We know from Revelation 12:9 that Satan has been cast out of Heaven and has fallen on the earth. Therefore, we live in a fallen, sin-filled, and perverse world. We are literally in the middle of Satan's playing ground. And Satan hates God's children. We represent something that he'll never have; an intimate relationship with the Father.

As a result, he roams about like a roaring lion, seeking whom he may devour 1 Peter 5:8. The devil is thirsty for God's children. The adversary desperately wants to sink his teeth into the hearts and minds of God's people. He wishes to derail them and take them further away from God. Indeed, if Satan were able to, he'd have all who confess Jesus Christ, sitting right next to him in hell.

Because of this, we're warned to be sober and vigilant so that we can resist the devil while remaining steadfast in the faith. And when we walk with a sober mind, we walk with more clarity and understand spiritual things better.

*Prayer Tool*

In truth, having eyes that can perceive beyond the natural, enforces our artillery as we pray in the Spirit. Whether we perceive with our natural mind or spiritual sight, we must have language. We must know how to pray.

Still, even if we may not always know what we're praying for or why we're praying, our spirit does. Hence, praying in tongues is a powerful prayer worship tool that all believers must activate and use.

## *Prayer Tool*

*Let us pray for the activation and maturation of our Spiritual Language*

Father, I thank You for being a sweet and loving Father. Lord, I repent of all known and unknown sins. Father, I desire to be conformed to Your image. So, Lord, I ask that You purge me of everything resisting your will. Conform me to the image of Christ.

Lord, I thank You that You're a Father who cares for His children. Lord God, in Jesus' name, I will utter all Words You've given me. So, Father, by faith and with boldness, I ask for the gift of speaking in tongues. Lord, I also ask that You increase the gift of tongues within me.

Father, I declare that I am Your child and You've given me spiritual sight to see in the spiritual and natural. Father, in Jesus' name, I declare that I will no longer stifle your voice, for I will not quench the Holy Spirit. I will proclaim Your will even the more. I will shout Your praises, even LOUDER. For Father, I am not ashamed of the gifts and the love that You've given me. By faith, I will activate and use all Your gifts.

Father, In Jesus' name, I thank You for the powerful gift of speaking in tongues. In Jesus' name, Lord, I thank You for Your Holy Spirit. Amen.

## Chapter | 5

## Prayers That Breaks the Yoke

*E*arly in my walk with God, the Lord led me to an entire year of weekly fasting and praying. Even more, during some weeks, I was led to a longer fast. Very seldom does a babe in Christ take on an immense challenge of intense fasting.

Therefore, I believed that such fast was to increase my faith and strengthen my walk. So, I fasted eagerly with much zeal and excitement. During that time, the Lord started opening my spiritual eyes.

## Prayer Tool

I remember receiving revelation about things only those who'd studied and grown for years would've known and received. It was almost like the Holy Spirit Himself interpreted scriptures and its deep meanings to me. For me, that year was a time of refreshing and strengthening.

Towards the end of my fast, I received a personal prophecy which alluded to John 13:7, "What I am doing you do not understand now, but you will know after this." I had no idea that I was getting ready to be immersed in a whirlwind of isolation, rejection, and even persecution, particularly from the *church*. As a new believer, spiritually, it was a trying time for me. I was hurt, confused, scared, fearful, and doubtful to the point that I wanted nothing to do with the church. I stayed away for months.

However, after my time of separation, I was still in the same spiritual warfare and very lonely. Though, much like David, the Lord sought after me in my cave of rejection. It was in those loneliest times that the Lord began ministering to my heart and continued to assure me that I am His child, and He has chosen me. In addition, He then revealed the major reason why I was called to a year-long fast.

God saw the attacks and persecution that were ahead. Therefore, the purpose of the fast was to partner with the Lord as my angels fought my battles. The fast also prepared my spirit for much-needed endurance. We must realize that we are called to walk in obedience even if we're unsure as to why.

I genuinely believe that if I yield to my flesh and denied the call of fasting, spiritually, I would have fallen on hard grounds. However, that fast taught me how to trust the Lord. During those times when I wanted to give-up and eat, I learned to fuel on God's Word and allow it to digest into my spirit. I learned how to become dependent on the Spirit of the Lord and allow Him to nourish me daily.

As a result, I began talking back to the enemy. Whenever Satan said something about me, I declared that I was NOT and whenever he called out my name, I proclaimed who I was in Christ even louder. I learned how to use the Word of God as my weapon against tormenting thoughts that tried to keep me in bondage. I also learned how to lean on the Lord and not lean on my understanding. Therefore, an attack of that magnitude that could've resulted in me separating from the body of Christ for years and possibly a lifetime only lasted for a few months.

Honestly, I can only attribute my long-suffering and steadfastness to fasting. It's only by the Grace of God that I was able to tap into my spiritual arsenal and fight back. We, as believers, must get into the habit of fasting unto the Lord. For fasting allows you to partner with the Holy Spirit as He fights your battles. Fasting breaks barriers, and fine-tune your spirit into proper alignment with the Father. Fasting also prepares your spirit-man for attacks, both present and those to come. Most importantly, fasting matures you and brings you into full spiritual stature.

### Fast unto the Lord

Because we are spiritual beings living in earthen vessels, fasting is paramount. All believers need to make fasting part their lives. Fasting is a form of honoring and submitting our will to God. A Fast unto the Lord is an expression of humility and worship. When it comes to fasting, God honors a heart posture that is not self-seeking nor one that seeks the attention of others. When we fast, we are to do so in our 'closet,' privately.

Typically, when the Lord designates an entire chapter in the Bible about a subject, He must means business. Isaiah 58 talks about God's desires and thoughts concerning how we fast in comparison to how fasting should be done.

The Lord starts the chapter with a clarion call. He poured out His heart in tears towards a generation who claims to desire to seek Him, yet their actions say otherwise. Thus, He sent His messengers to declare and pave the way in which they should walk. Likewise, the same is true for our generation. God has looked at the habits of our fasting and is calling us higher and drawing us deeper into Him.

As God examined the hearts of the Generation in Isaiah and our generation, He notices how in our seeking and pursuit of Him, some have grown weary. In verses 2-3 of Isaiah 58, the Lord says, "Yet they seek Me daily, and delight to know My ways... they delight in approaching God. Why have we fasted, they say, and You have not seen? Why have we afflicted our souls, and You take no notice?" These two scriptures highlight a generation who have grown tired of fasting.

Often when burnouts and weariness occur, it tends to result from wrong motives, whether intentionally or not. In pursuing God, it's easy for one to seek diligently and end up in fatigue, which usually results from discouragement. At times, it may feel as if God is not moving fast enough or as if He's forgotten you. Likewise, such feelings can come about while fasting and not seeing the desired results.

However, getting to the root of why you're fasting will help alleviate potential discouragement. Most often, when we fast, it's usually because of a need or desire. We tend to fast when we're searching for a breakthrough, the desire to grow, and even because we feel as if we must. However, the most troubling thing about fasting for these reasons is that the chances of your heart posture falling out of alignment with the Father is high. While fasting to increase in faith and even to receive a breakthrough is perfectly fine and quite frankly common, we must evaluate our stance.

As we fast, it's ideal to ponder on heart searching questions as it establishes a foundation for your fast. Such questions can trigger thoughts concerning your heart and willingness to engage in warfare alongside Heaven. Questions like; what is God's will for this area of my life? Will it be a detriment if I don't receive my petition? Can I endure a length of time while waiting for my answered prayers? Do I have the grit to fight in faith, prayer, and go to war during and after this fast? Or, will I become contentious towards God, if my expectations are not met? These are merely some questions that should be asked and answered while journeying through your fast.

When it comes to the children of Israel, they faulted while fasting, which produced discouragement. They had wrong motives, and they began to doubt their purpose of consecrating themselves. They figured what was the point if they did not see their intended breakthrough. Sadly, many of us have the same thoughts concerning fasting. We've forgotten to consider the Lord. However, we must get back to the basics.

It's crucial that we go beyond our flesh and seek the heart of the Father. When we consider the Lord in our lives, we understand that His ways are not our ways, nor is His timeframe ours. Therefore, we must become content in whatever outcome we receive.

Above all else, fasting draws us closer to the Lord and strengthens our spiritual sight. Fasting also reveals the content of our hearts and purifies us. Starting in verse three, the Lord revealed that the children of Israel fasted to please their flesh, and their hearts were wicked. As a result, God chastised them. More often than none, when you fast, it'll bring your impurities to the forefront. However, when this happens, God is showing you your posture so you can make the necessary adjustments. As God stated, "you will not fast as you do this day" Isaiah 58:4.

When God chastises, His goal is to correct. Though the children of Israel were chastised, He also showed them the proper way in which He delights in fasting. Starting off, the Lord broke down their ideology concerning fasting. Usually, when God wants to show you the state of your heart, He typically does so with a question. Therefore, the Lord asked, "Is it a fast that I have chosen, a day for a man to afflict his soul? Is it to bow down his head like a bulrush, and to spread out sackcloth and ashes? Would you call this a fast, and an acceptable day to the Lord?" Isaiah 58:5. The purpose of the Lord asking these questions is to get to the root of the matter.

The Lord is asking, have you designated a day you consider 'fasting' to afflict your soul in pity, and have you followed rituals and customs to add a check to your checklist? When we fast, it should be a delight in our spirit. And likewise, it should not be as a result of following the crowd but rather a genuine heartfelt desire to please and seek the Lord.

Fasting deals with the spirit and heart of matters; therefore, the Lord shows us how we should fast. In verse 6, the Lord leads with a follow-up question, "Is this not the fast that I have chosen: To loose the bonds of wickedness, to undo the heavy burdens, to let the oppressed go free, and that you break every yoke? Is it not to share your bread with the hungry…?" The purpose of God's follow-up questions was to reveal His wisdom concerning His will and way as it pertains to His fast.

When we fast the Lord's way, we declare with an understanding that we are operating in the spiritual realm. We fast to bind and rebuke evil spirits and principalities that are keeping the children of God captive and in bondage. As we fast, our heart posture is in humility because we know that the battles we're facing are already won. Therefore, we're able to walk in humility and share the love of Christ as Jesus loved. We walk with clarity and understanding that though we're fasting, it's not a day where we are to isolate ourselves nor show and prove to the world that we're fasting, but rather walk with the spirit of servanthood.

Because fasting deals with the spiritual elements, we must understand that our flesh, feelings, and emotions must be removed from the equation. We must continually apply 2 Corinthians 10:5 to our lives. Whenever we feel ourselves wavering and feeding into our fleshly desires, then we must bring every thought captive under the obedience and submission of Jesus Christ. Fasting is a major deal. Strongholds are pulled down, burdens are lifted, lives are saved, and nations are transformed into the image of God. Therefore, it should be taken seriously as it's holy, sacred, and life-changing to the Lord.

## As we pray

Fasting is one of the most powerful arsenals you could ever use. However, you create dynamite while combining it with praying. Yet, many are not privy to this truth because it's spiritual. As we fast and pray, we activate a spiritual eruption that disrupts the kingdom of darkness. In fact, when you fast and pray, all of hell is vexed because you've interfered with the enemy's agenda.

We must become aggressive with our spiritual warfare, as the kingdom of heaven suffers violence, and the violent takes it by force, Matthew 11:12. When we gird ourselves in the Spirit of the Lord, we become violent by not accepting hell's verdict but instead fighting back to stand for the Kingdom of Heaven. The proper way to fight back is to stand firm in the Lord. When you stand in God, you cannot be wavered nor swayed to the left because His armor allows you to stand against the wiles of the devil, Ephesians 6:11. However, you can only reap the benefits of His armor by abiding in Him.

When you abide in God, your eyes are open to the truth of God's Word. Because of such, you can stand on the Word of God, and declare it over your life. Declaring God's truth over your life and situation is called girding your waist with truth. When you're girded with the truth, your foundation is rooted in God, and the Lord is your sustainer. Though you may experience attacks and setbacks, you won't waver from the truth of God, because it's established in you.

Likewise, because you've planted yourself in Christ, you can put on His righteousness. To have the righteousness of Jesus is to walk blameless before the Lord. Therefore, when the enemy tries to accuse you, you're only recovered by the grace of the Holy Spirit. God's grace says that He remembers your faults no more. God's grace emphasis the truth that in Him, you're a new creation; therefore, your walk and faith in Christ is no match for the devil. Through abiding in Christ and living under His righteousness, you're complete and sealed by the Holy Spirit.

Because the Holy Spirit seals you, you should walk with the peace of Jesus. The peace of Jesus is knowing His testimony to be true. Just like Jesus, though you may be accused, attacked, and hard-pressed, you're at peace knowing that The Great Redeemer has already conquered all your battles, and the foe is defeated. Therefore, the peace of Jesus surpasses your understanding for your hope is established in Christ.

However, above all else, you must be shielded with faith. As you walk in faith, the Holy Spirit ensures that your actions and words agree with your belief. Your actions must agree with your faith because, without faith, it's impossible to please God Hebrews 11:6. For your faith is the conduit to Heaven's breakthrough and God's glory over your life. Through faith, you transcend spiritually. As a result, the enemy must back off you, in Jesus' name. Your faith is what confirms you in the Lord as you walk boldly and confidently for God's

Kingdom and Glory. Most importantly, your faith shields you from the devil as the Holy Spirit validates your covenant with Christ. For by faith, we are saved through Christ Jesus.

Also, as children of God, we must remember that we are Christ's. We must allow our identity in Him to cover our minds as we use the Word of God to pull down strongholds and everything that exalts itself against the knowledge of God 2 Corinthians 10:5. Our Helmet of Salvation checks our train of thought and places them under the submission of Jesus. Every idle word and every thought that's outside of God's intentions must be brought down in Jesus' name. Your mind must be fixated on Jesus as it'll keep your feet grounded as you work out your salvation with fear and trembling Philippians 2:12.

The last physical piece of the Armor is the Sword of the Spirit. The Sword of the Spirit is the Word of God. As we're praying, tearing down strongholds, breaking generational curses, and even calling forth generational blessings, we must use the Word of God. We must declare God's Words over our lives. We must meditate on the scriptures and allow God's promises to take root in our soul. As we allow the Word of God to consume us, we become walking and talking weapons, because God's Word is living and powerful, and sharper than two-edged sword Hebrews 4:12.

As you put on the Armor of God, prayer should never leave you. The Lord instructs us to pray without ceasing, which means we must always consider the thoughts of the Lord. We must remain in

*Prayer Tool*

constant connection with God. There should never come a time where the circuit that connects us to Heaven is cut. You must therefore continuously keep prayer on your lips. While you're praying you must also remain watchful for the move of God and endure with His fruit of long-suffering.

## *Prayer Tool*

As mentioned, fasting is paramount, and when incorporating prayer, it's dynamite. Moreover, when wearing God's Armor, you become fully equipped and loaded with all spiritual artillery that's needed for successful combat. Therefore, our Prayer Tool is focused on praying on the full Armor of God.

**Father,**

In Jesus name, I bless You. Lord, I thank You. For Father, You are the Almighty, the Great I AM. Father, You alone are worthy to be praised, so I praise Your name. Father, I repent and ask that You forgive my sins and trespasses as I forgive others.

Lord God, I ask that You give me full provision as I put on Your full Armor. Lord, with your clothing, I am fully equipped and protected from the wiles of the devil. For Lord, I know I must remain fully clothed because I wrestle not against flesh and blood but against principalities, against powers, against rulers of the darkness of this age, and against spiritual host of wickedness in the heavenly places.

Therefore, I will gird my waist as I walk in Your truth, while the Holy Spirit covers me with the breastplate of righteousness. Father, I thank You for allowing me to shod my feet with the sweet preparation of the Gospel of Peace for, by it, I am saved. Father, I declare that from this day forward, I walk confidently with my shield of faith, for I know You alone have called and chosen me. So, father, I will walk tall and wear my helmet of salvation that You've given me. I will continually present myself as a living sacrifice holy and acceptable unto You.

Father, though I may be hard-pressed, I am not destroyed, for your Word is my sword. Therefore, I remain in constant contact with You by prayer and supplication. In Jesus' name, Holy Spirit help me to remain watchful. Amen. - Ephesians 6:11-18

## Chapter | 6

## Prayers That Break the Powers

*O*ne of the most important truth we must know as Blood bought believers is the authority and access, we have for pulling down strongholds and breaking the powers of principalities. Through the Blood and power of Jesus, we must stand in faith and walk in the authority that Christ has given us. Sadly, many believers undergo unnecessary suffering due to their lack of faith.

However, Jesus tells us in John 14:12 that greater works we will do because He goes to the Father. Is Jesus serious with *Greater works*? Yes! Once we grasp the true meaning of His statement, then can we confidently break yokes and unauthorize every principality.

In 2 Kings 4:8-37, we saw highlights of one of many stories in the Bible where prayer broke the powers of principalities. Prayer broke the power of death. It was the story of a Shunammite woman who desired to serve and honor Elisha, a great prophet of God. Elisha acknowledged the woman's desire to serve and honor him and had compassion towards her. As a gesture of appreciation, Elisha asked if there was anything he could do to show gratitude.

In response to Elisha's request, Gehazi, Elisha's servant said that the woman has no child, and her husband is old. Elisha being a prophet, activated her womb by using his prophetic anointing and declared that she would bear a son. As soon as the prophetic word went forth, within a year, the Shunammite woman conceived and had a son.

However, when her son was still young, he became ill and died. Out of desperation, this woman sought after Elisha the prophet. She hoped for healing and the revival of her son. Once the Shunammite woman shared her problem with Elisha, he instructed his servant, Gehazi, to run ahead of him and go to the woman's house. *Why this instruction?*

Gehazi was to place Elisha's staff on the boy's face. The purpose of the staff was to anoint and revive the Shunammite's son.

However, it failed. You know, I then discover that a powerful weapon in the hand of a faithless man is always rendered powerless!

Now, Elisha had to go himself. When Elisha got to the woman's house, he demanded that everyone leave the room so he could be alone with the dead boy. While Elisha was with the Shunammite's dead son, he prayed fervently and heeded the voice of the Lord. In prayers, you must be ready to listen constantly to God's instructions or directions.

Prophetically as a sign of life, Elisha repeatedly breathe upon the young boy and afterwards stretched his body on him. Isn't that looking foolish and stupid? God doesn't need to be logical with us before He is obeyed. After moments of prayer and the prophetic act, Elisha broke the power of death and the grave. The boy came back to life.

The Shunammite woman knew where the oil of the Lord was and she looked for it. She also understood the power of faith. Therefore, she rejected the verdict of death, and through determination she received her *alive* son. The forces that wanted her son dead were broken!

Thankfully, the oil of the Lord flows beyond Elisha and the Shunammite woman. You have the same access to the Power of the Lord. While there's no cookie-cutter formula through which we can activate such authority, it's important we note that it is only through service, determination, faith, and fervent prayer that the power of hell is broken.

I wonder what powers you're allowing to rule your life due to lack of faith. Are you accepting a verdict of death because you fear the chances of life? Surprisingly, though most proclaim life, many are afraid of living.

They never believe the possibility of life after death, so they would rather accept death than believe God. However, we must break that thinking and have faith even in the smallest part of our life.

I believe some instances that are deemed dead may remain, but I also know that there are many areas in our lives where God wishes to resurrect. However, we must apply more of faith than we do fear. We must go beyond our natural lenses and seek the face and authority of Jesus. We must believe that there is power in the name of Jesus, and should we call on Him, then He is faithful to save, resurrect, and even heal.

## *Who are you consulting?*

The Shunammite woman knew that the survival of her son was a matter of life and death, and that spirits and principalities must be stopped. Therefore, she didn't consult just anybody or make negative confessions. She took the case to a reputable man of faith knowing that should her son have a chance to live, then a man of God needed to intervene.

However, we shouldn't get caught up on the fact that it was a man of God but rather the Spirit of God that she chose to follow. The Shunammite woman decided to honor and seek the voice of God. She shut all avenues that could've had the chance of sowing seeds of fear and doubt in her.

It's important that as believers in Jesus Christ, we're casting down imaginations that are contrary to the Word of God. We must consider whose voice we're consulting. Are we taking heed to a false fate, false doctrine, fear, pride, shame, and even insecurity? Or are we breathing life in all areas of our lives? Are we blessing our families with the Word of faith? And are we using the Word of God as our Armor?

### *It's not flesh and blood*

2 Corinthians 10:3-10 tells us that our battles are within the unseen realm. Therefore, we must fight having this understanding.

It would be crazy and absurd to choose a pillow as a form of weaponry to fight in a combat. Pillows are best used for sleeping, which is a physical engagement. Why will a soldier carry a pillow to the battlefield when machine guns are best for wars. It is the battle you're faced with that determines your weaponry. Hence, we must know that our battle is not physical but spiritual.

Therefore, the "weapons of our warfare should *never* carnal but mighty in God for pulling down of strongholds. We must cast down arguments and every high thing that exalts itself against the knowledge of God" (2 Corinthians 10:3-5 emphasis added).

We must take authority over every thought and bring it under the obedience of Jesus Christ. Also, we must be diligent in walking in obedience. As we saw in our last chapter, putting on Christ's righteousness is needed for us to be blameless before Him. Equally, we must walk in the obedience of Jesus.

When facing battles in the unseen realm, there will be numerous accusations against you. Therefore, the Holy Spirit must be there for you as your Comforter. However, walking in disobedience and unrighteousness gives a legal access for the enemy to attempt an attack on you.

Therefore, you must present yourself to Jesus. Even though we must present ourselves blameless before the Lord, in our natural state, we can never do so. We must first submit our lives to Christ and allow Him to renew us into His image.

Being renewed into the image of God means sitting at the feet of Jesus and allowing His Spirit to work and dwell in you. As the Holy Spirit abides in you, each day, you are being transformed into the image of God. It's only in the presence of the Lord that we're immersed and strengthened with authority to fight our spiritual battles.

## In Christ's Authority

Acts chapter 19 highlights the use of unauthorized power. There were seven sons of Sceva who attempted to cast out evil spirits in Jesus' name. However, the evil spirits questioned their authority and asked; "Jesus I know, and Paul I know; but who are you?" Acts 19:15 These seven sons of Sceva lacked authority and a working relationship with Jesus; as a result, the evil spirits knew they were unauthorized and overpowered them.

It would be shameful to try to break yokes and tear down strongholds with a lack of relationship and the authority from Jesus. The powers and principalities of this age would not succumb to your efforts and gimmicks.

Daniel, from the Old Testament, understood the importance of this. In Daniel chapters 1 through 3, Daniel chose to stand in faith and never spoil himself with sin.

During Daniels' time, he and many other young men were brought to Babylon to serve King Nebuchadnezzar. Shortly after, king Nebuchadnezzar made a decree that everyone must bow to a golden image and serve his gods. There was a fiery furnace for anyone who dared to disobey the king's decree.

Daniel's friends decided never to bow nor worship the golden image. Therefore, king Nebuchadnezzar condemned Daniel's friends to death. They were thrown in the furnace and was supposed to be killed, but God! The Almighty One was there to keep them safe.

In Daniel chapter three, verse 24, the king's eyes were opened and he asked a question to confirm if they sent more than three boys into the furnace. However, in verse 25, we saw that even though there were three men thrown into the fire, there was a fourth man there to save them and make sure not a hair on their bodies was torched.

The fourth man was the Spirit of God and because Daniel and His friends did to not defile themselves, God honored their faithfulness and commitment. God saw fit to save them because they were men who decide to remain set apart and sacred before Him. Daniel and his three Hebrew friends honored the Spirit of God over graven images and foreign gods. As a result, in times of need, God continuously stepped in.

There will come a time in your walk with God where you must choose whose authority you'll follow. My prayer is that you'll look beyond your barriers and trust God more. I pray that over everything, you'll stand for Christ.

Just like Daniel and his friends, the road to honoring God may not always be easy; you'll have major hurdles that you'll be required to overcome. Yet, much like the three Hebrew boys, you're never alone. Even in your darkest and hardest battles, Jesus is always there.

*Can He trust you?*

After Daniel's numerous acts of obedience, God noted that Daniel could be trusted. Therefore, Daniel and his friends were granted the opportunity to serve alongside the king in his palace. In addition, Daniel's gifts became a tool for making his God known. Daniel and his friends were promoted after the interpretation of the king's dream. It's incredible that even in the most trying situation, God's glory was magnified. God is looking for a nation that will bear His heart and consider His ways. He's looking for individuals whom He can trust with His power.

Because God could trust Daniel, He increased his spiritual stature. Daniels' heavenly gifts were multiplied, and fasting and interceding became his lifestyle. As Daniel was elevated, he remained adamant about not bowing down, nor serving the Babylonian gods. Daniel knew the importance of considering God's will over his own will. Daniel knew that despite the challenges he faced, there was a greater task that must be fulfilled. Therefore, he fasted as he was led and God gave him prophetic dreams and vision.

*Will you Travail?*

Daniel chapter 10 emphasizes the importance of dying to self so that God's will prevails. After an intense message, Daniel immediately felt a burden in his spirit to intercede. This he did with weeping, mourning, and fasting. He travailed. Because Daniel bore the heartbeat of God, he was able to put aside his natural lenses and fight in the spiritual. Daniel knew that what was revealed was an attempt of spiritual domination from the wicked principalities; therefore, he fought a spiritual battle.

However, this spiritual battle was like no other. For twenty-one days, Daniel fasted and prayed. Daniel was weak yet persistent to the point that an angel of the Lord appeared to him to give him answers to his prayers. God knew that Daniel could've experienced frustration, weariness, and even uncertainty if anything would break or stop due to the effect of his prayers.

Therefore, God sent His angel, to encourage and inform him that the powers he was fasting and praying against, fought back for twenty-one days. The answers had been released from heaven from the first day but it was hindered by the spiritual forces. Persistence in praying secured Daniel's victory! Just because Daniel was fasting and praying, there was battle in the heavenly realm. We, as believers, must understand the significance of bearing a heart like Jesus in fasting and praying till we are transfigured and our answers delivered.

Many of us are believing God for something but those things we're believing God for might be held up. Sadly, many of us give up too soon.

Sometimes a delay simply means waiting for God, or much like Daniel, a delay could be the result of spiritual warfare. Therefore, though we may be uncertain of the reasons for a delay, but we must never relax too quickly in the place of prayer. We must remain readily available to posture ourselves in prayer, even if it appears as if nothing is happening.

It's through our fasting and praying that we build an intense and in-depth relationship with Christ. It's through fasting and praying that we subdue the flesh and renew our strength to fight our spiritual battles.

Though we're human and still in our bodies, we are spirit beings living and operating in and from the spiritual realm. Therefore, it's important that we develop a fasting and praying lifestyle. Numerous scriptures testifies, our fight is never natural, nor is it with other humans. So, whether we believe it or not, everything originates in the spirit. The spiritual governs the physical!

Moreover, we must gird ourselves with the Word of God. We must clothe ourselves in His full armor and engage in this spiritual battle, for it's the only way in which our prayers can break the powers.

## *Prayer Tool*

*Our prayer target is focused on an increased level of a fasting and praying lifestyle.*

**Father,**

In Jesus' name, You are Holy. You are our true and loving Father. Lord, I bless Your name. Father, I ask that You continue to purify my heart and teach me how to sanctify myself as I fast before You. Lord, I desire to mature spiritually while growing closer to You. So, Father, I ask that You lead me to be more consecrated to a sanctified lifestyle through fasting and praying. Lead me into a lifestyle that is pleasing to You.

In Jesus name, I declare that through my fasting and praying, chains and evil powers are broken. Father I declare that through my fasting and praying Your perfect love and peace is revealed. In Jesus' name, I pray Amen.

## Chapter 7

## Declare, and it shall be

*I* wonder why the Lord said, without faith, it's impossible to please Him; could it be that faith is Heaven's currency? Or is it that faith opens the communication device that connects us to Christ? Perhaps, just maybe, faith really does move mountains? Well, I believe all this is true. Therefore, faith is the predecessor for all things related to Christ and the Kingdom. It's no wonder why in Hebrews 11:6, it was noted that without faith, it's impossible to please God.

As believers of Christ, when in prayer, we declare the will of the Father by exercising our authority in faith. To see the things of God unfold, we must press-in, in unwavering faith.

I would never forget the time when I was in elementary school, and we had a field day. Towards the end of the event, the school was conducting drawings for numerous prizes. I remember thinking that I had never won anything, and I would really like to win. Lo-and-behold, my name was called, and I won a bike! I know in my spirit that my faith connected with Heaven and pulled on the heartstrings of God. As a result, my prayer was answered.

It amazes me that at such a tender age, I understood the power of faith. Though I was unsure of my outcome, I had a strong desire. I knew in my heart that I wanted to win. So, I didn't give a second thought to the other potential winners. Therefore, by faith, I prayed and believed that I would receive it. I did.

While walking in faith, you may not always be sure of the outcome. However, faith requires us to look past the variables of uncertainty. We must not glorify our doubts nor allow seeds of fear to be planted within our hearts. Most importantly, we mustn't allow doubt to manifest in our future. Instead, we should place our hope in the goodness of Jesus. We should trust that even in uncertainties, the Lord is still looking to honor our faith.

## *Your unwavering Faith*

There was a time where the disciples were operating in the gifts of healing and miracles. According to their track record, they had the power of Jesus backing their efforts when they rebuked demons and ushered miraculous healings.

Despite the disciples' capabilities, there was a man who requested Jesus to heal his epileptic son, because the disciples could not cure him. As a result, Jesus remarked that we're a 'faithless and perverse generation' Matthew 17:17. Jesus knew that if the disciples applied more pressure in faith, then they could've cast out the demonic spirit of epilepsy.

Even further, there are areas in our lives where Jesus is waiting for our faith. For the Lord said, if our faith is comparable to the smallest seed, a mustard seed, then we can move mountains. To have faith the size of a mustard seed is applying faith into a definite possibility, versus accepting a verdict that rejects all hope.

Faith as the size of a mustard seed, and having faith amid everything that defiles favor, can get God to produce exceedingly, abundantly above all that *you* ask or think Ephesians 3:20.

When you step outside your environment of faith and boldness, and you venture into the 'just maybe' side of the equation. God will beat your curiosity and meet you right in the middle with your desired miracles. The Lord wants to see that you're applying some work along with your faith, by taking one step at a time.

To have unwavering faith does not mean that you're void of reservations. Even Jesus asked if His cup of suffering and agonies can be taken from Him.

On numerous occasions, David pleaded with the Lord. When being sentenced to the furnace, Daniel proclaimed that the Lord would deliver them, with the same breath that agreed with the chances of not being delivered.

No, unwavering faith does not mean that you're void of reservations. On the contrary, unwavering faith implies that despite your outcomes, your confidence and trust are in God alone.

Unwavering faith yields to god-favoring possibilities. To have steadfast faith is to know that there are verdicts that are contrary to God's beliefs and desires, but you'll never invest your time. You understand that spending your time in anything contrary to God's knowledge, breeds discontent, confusion, and frustration. Therefore, your faith in Christ is the foundation upon which God builds your life.

Indeed, God is most pleased when you have unwavering faith. Exercising unwavering faith not only proves your trust in Him but also solidifies your firm belief in Him. For the Lord says, 'Now faith is the substance of things hoped for, the evidence of things not seen' Hebrews 11:1.

When it comes to building our relationship with God, it takes faith. We must have faith to believe in His existence as we cannot physically see Him. Even further, as we wait on Christ, our faith must be rooted in His Word. We must believe that if God declared a thing, then it shall be.

It would be foolish of us to pray, declare, and decree if we lacked faith. Like I said earlier, we are spirit beings operating and living within a spiritual realm. A realm that we could never see with our natural lenses; therefore, we need faith as we pray and declare bold decrees.

While God's Word stands on its own, when we partner with Heaven, our faith becomes the conduit that ushers God's will into our lives and situations. And of course, many assignments and blessings are attached to your name, being God's elect. However, your faith is the driving force that will cause you to attain them. Therefore, in all things, God requires our faith.

### Giant-Sized Faith

I'm pretty sure you heard the saying, 'your eyes are bigger than your stomach.' Well, this saying was true for the children of Israel.

There was a time when King Saul made a humongous mistake. While he reigned in Israel, the king thought he was bigger and bolder than his reality.

## Prayer Tool

It happened that King Saul and his men had a brilliant idea to position themselves before the Philistines. And although the Philistines had more giants and military might than the children of Israel, yet, Saul figured through the lens of a giant-sized faith that Israel could take them on in combat. Whereas, in the mind of the Philistines, the children of Israel were no match for them.

Goliath, who was a fierce giant of the Philistines', approached the army of Israel and questioned why they started a war when the Philistines are more than capable of killing them off at the snap of a finger.

Also, Goliath gave them a proposition. If a single man from their army can kill him, then the Philistines would become the children of Israel's servants. On the contrary, if the children of Israel are defeated, then they would become servants to the Philistines.

Goliath took Saul and his army for a joke. He knew the Children of Israel could never stand a chance against his team. Therefore, he mocked them, saying, 'I defy the armies of Israel.'

Even though Saul proclaimed against the Philistines, after he heard the remarks from Goliath, he retreated. Saul and the children Israel became filled with fear and regretted standing against them. Saul knew that Goliath meant business, and reasoned that his life and the population of his people were in jeopardy.

You must understand the magnitude of a declaration. When you declare, everything yields, and much like the Philistines, those things that are to yield may show resistance. You must, however, stand firm as you sustain your faith.

Faith-filled declarations are a matter of life and death, leading to fulfillment or stagnation, winning the battle, or standing in defeat. When you're declaring the Word of God, there's no room for fear.

Fear is a dangerous tool to put to use. Due to worry, the children of Israel lives were at stake. However, if Saul and his men remained tenacious and continued with boldness, chances are the Lord would have delivered the Philistines into their hands. Instead, you must hold on to your giant-sized faith, even amid impossibilities.

While the men of Israel were in disarray, one man understood the power and importance of a declaration. Young David, who wasn't old enough to fight in battle, stood with holy indignation when he heard of Goliath's antagonizing remarks. David couldn't fathom the thought of someone who wasn't a child of God, defeat the children of God. Therefore, He stepped forward.

David, being filled with much zeal, declared that no uncircumcised Philistine would defy the armies of the Lord. David, unlike Saul and his men, was firm with his decrees. He sealed his declaration with faith. He knew that the same God who stood by him in various tests and tribulations would stand by him and deliver him

*Prayer Tool*

again. David never saw a giant-sized Philistine. Instead, he saw a giant-sized, faithful God.

Though David knew the importance of faith-filled declarations, he also understood the mandate of backing your faith with works. He, therefore, rejected Goliath's aggressive appearance and chose to battle with him.

In preparation, David grabbed a few stones and his slingshot. Though Goliath had a sword, David ran full force towards Goliath and slung his sling, knocking him to the ground. David then grabbed Goliath's sword and finished him off by decapitating his head.

Though everything around David screamed that defeating his enemy was impossible, he remembered God. David stood firm in his declarations and believed with full faith when he decreed that, 'the battle is the Lord's and He will give *the Philistines* into *their* hands,' 1 Samuel 17:47.

As a result, God moved in response to his faith, and David prevailed. God is waiting to advance in your life, but He must find you faithful. Your faith is the transmitter to God moving on your behalf.

As God finds you faithful over an area of your life, He will then open many 'faith' doors in various areas. Every faith door that you walk through will require you to stretch your faith in Jesus. You will be required to trust God in all circumstances as you remember all that God has done for you.

Definitely, the road and process of exercising such faith and trust in God may not always be easy. So, holding on to God's faithfulness is imperative as you walk through every faith door and test within your journey.

## *It Still Remains*

Because David remained faithful in all his ways, the Lord promised that he'd become king over Israel. Initially, David didn't have a direct link to royalty. However, God saw fit and made him king.

There will be times where you may never qualify for a door that God is opening. It is your faithfulness to God that better equips you for what He is about to do in your life. Yet, much like David, you may have to endure as you traverse.

After David defeated Goliath, his name became adored throughout Israel. As a result, many women danced and sung proclamations that 'Saul has slain his thousands, and David his ten thousands 1 Samuel 18:7.

As king, when Saul heard the sayings, he became filled with furious anger and envy. At every chance, Saul sought to kill David.

*Prayer Tool*

He couldn't grasp the thought of a young boy pulling rank. As a result, David's life was in jeopardy, he became fearful and ran.

Although God revealed His faithfulness through the defeat of Goliath, David could not see past himself nor the threat to his life. Therefore, he hid in caves.

Many have forgotten that God remains faithful. Sadly, we (I say 'we' because I too was in this same boat) resort to retreating and hiding out in 'caves.' We believe that self-medicated remedies such as isolation will remove the threat over our lives and purposes. Unfortunately, it does not. Because caves represent isolation, casting yourself away can open many doors for the enemy.

The devil loves open doors as he walks about like a roaring lion, seeking whom he may devour 1 Peter 5:8. Therefore, it's essential to understand that being separated from God or his children means being disconnected from the Source or people who might encourage and impart wisdom and knowledge. It's during isolation that Satan takes the opportunity to have a field day on the minds of God's people. So, we must remain vigilant.

However, because caves are a representation of isolation, it's also the perfect time for God to commune with you and heal you. What you have to do is be receptive to the call and move of the Lord. As David was in hiding, he became a leader over a few hundred who were broken in spirit. David attracted people who were like him, in need of healing and hope.

Yet, as much as the people were drawn to David, he understood the importance of reassurance. He knew that sticking close to God was paramount for his survival. Therefore, the declaration of life was always on his lips.

Often, when a leader is being attacked spiritually, those who are under their covering will face a degree of attacks. Thus, as David's life was being threatened, he assured his people that although those who seek to kill him, are now trying to kill them, under his covering, they are safe.

As David proclaimed life over himself, he knew that as a leader, he must also proclaim life over his people. Most times, God calls us not only to declare liberty for ourselves, but also for those who are in our midst. God is calling us to stretch our faith to those who are of little faith.

Ironically, after David proclaimed safety, Saul continued hunting him. And so, once again, David ran. Nonetheless, a perpetual cycle of Saul chasing David and David running from Saul was inevitable. As David and his men retreated either to a cave, city, or stronghold, some spies always tipped Saul off.

Much like any situation, you cannot run your entire life. There will be a point in time where God will make you confront your offender head-on.

Your time in caves is supposed to be the moments where God nurtures your soul. Caves are meant to repair you, comfort you, create a boldness, and godly fear within you.

In truth, caves were never intended to keep you bound. Once you've sat at the feet of Jesus and received your healing and soul ministering, you're supposed to come out. You must come out of bondage and walk in your newfound freedom and boldness. Have faith that as you step out to confront whatever demonic spirit was trying to bind you, know that God is fighting for you. God will never leave you nor forsake you. As a child of God, your battle is always the Lord's.

When David ran out of places to hide, he was forced to confront Saul at every turn. On two occasions, David had the opportunity to kill Saul. Despite the chances to kill Saul and walk away freely, David had the understanding that Saul was still a child of God. Therefore, even though opportunities presented itself, David chose not to kill Saul. Instead, he proved his heart and loyalty to God. David was a fierce warrior of the Lord, so while he wanted to prove his heart, he also wanted to be clear that he is not to be messed with.

In 1 Samuel 24:11, while Saul was sleeping, David called out to him to show Saul how easy it was to cut the hem of his garment. Cutting the hem represented the power of authority and the ability to kill. Although Saul's countenance was down, David knew that should he take vengeance into his own hands, then there wouldn't be a battle for the Lord.

If God said vengeance is His, then we shouldn't wear Jesus' shoes, for if we do, then what place will He take in our troubles? We as believers must understand that when God fights our battles, most of the time, we're out of the equation. Our war cry is trusting in God, declaring life, and God's Words over ourselves.

## *Declare, and it Shall be*

We must note that through prayer, declaration, faith, and persistence, David escaped the hands of death. Even more so, due to David's obedience and acts of faith, God fought David's battle. 1 Samuel chapter 31 shows the second battle between Israel and the Philistines. Much like the first time, the children of Israel ran due to fear and intimidation. As a result, all of Israel, who ran from the Philistines, died except for Saul and his sons. Therefore, the Philistines chased them, killed Johnathan and his sons while leaving Saul gravely injured.

Saul couldn't fathom the thought of dying from wounds inflicted by a Philistine. Therefore, he fell on a sword killing himself.

The beauty of this ordeal is that David never had to come outside of God's character nor the parameters that God set forth. He remained true to his faith and honored God in all his ways.

As we bear the same record as David's, we'll begin to settle in the notion that God indeed fights our battles.

In all things, we must believe and use our faith tool and declare Psalm 142, just as David did. In the face of opposition, persecution, and even in good times, we must say that God is our refuge and our portion. We must always decree praise to the Lord, knowing that His righteousness surrounds us and that He deals bountifully with us.

*Armani D. White*

# *Prayer Tool*

*Let us declare and Decree God's Greatness over our lives*

### Declaration of Admiration

Father, You are the most wonderful God. Lord, I thank You for all that You've done. Lord, I trust that Your thoughts towards me are of good and not of evil. Father, I declare that I am the head and not the tail. I am above only and not beneath. Father, I declare that I am the apple of Your Eye. And Father, I stand firm in peace as I wait on You. Father, I declare that I have dove's eyes, always keeping my focus on You. Father, I proclaim that as I wait on You, You will renew my strength. Father, I have faith that I shall mount up on wings like eagles. Oh Lord, I shall run and not grow weary. Lord, I shall walk and not faint.

### Declaration of God's Faithfulness

Father, I testify that You do fight my battles, and Lord, You do go before me. Father, Your hands are forever on my life, watching and leading my every step. You've crafted me perfectly in Your image. Oh Lord, I decree that, in Jesus, I am complete and lacking nothing. I decree that as for me and my house, we shall praise You, oh Lord. For Father, You said that my house shall be blessed all the days of my life. So, Father, I declare that I am Your earthen treasure.

## Declaration of Blessings

Father, I thank You because I have peace that surpasses all my understanding. Lord, I declare that I am blessed. I am a blessing. My family is blessed. I am blessed in the city. I am blessed in my country; the fruits of my labor are blessed. My offspring are blessed. My home is blessed. Lord, I overflow with enriched blessings, and I expect great things. Father, I declare a financial blessing over my life. Father, I declare miraculous healing within my home. Lord, I press forth for I see Your hands breaking through in my life. Father, in Jesus' name, I declare and decree all great and Godly things follow me all the days of my life. In Jesus' name, I pray. Amen.

## Chapter 8

## Intercessors Arise

Earlier, I shared my story about my first Christian conference and the impact it had on my life.

In this chapter, I want to emphasize that the entire conference was beautiful. The nights were filled with so much passion for Christ as the glory of the Lord filled the place. I had never seen anything like that.

Under one roof, people were getting saved, filled with the Holy Ghost, delivered from demons, discovering their gifts, and so much more. I genuinely believe that this weekend was a crash course of everything Jesus from healing to spiritual warfare to miracles and deliverance ministry.

That day, my physical and spiritual eyes were open at the same time. I remember thinking I could stay there forever. I realized that God was so much larger than I thought. I wanted more of HIM!

However, after the first night's service, I was filled with so much excitement as I recalled everything that I had experienced. I was so stunned that as I started drifting off to sleep, I began hearing screams and wails. I heard all the torment and trauma of those who experienced deliverance; it was unsettling.

For hours I tossed and turned, trying to shake off those vehement yells, but I couldn't. So, I woke my roommate, whom I hardly knew. I told her I couldn't sleep, and instinctively she prayed, 'Father I thank You for sweet, sweet sleep in Jesus name, amen.'

Afterwards, she prayed, rolled over, and went back to sleep. I remember thinking, *that's it?* I was expecting more of an elaborate prayer with less tiredness and more force.

Surprisingly, though her prayer was the most straightforward and shortest prayer I'd ever receive to date, I woke up not knowing when I fell asleep. *Now, that was some sleep!*

Honestly, I believe there is something so profound about her simple yet effective prayer. I think we can all note the power of her intercession. When she interceded on my behalf, she did so automatically. She never second-guessed nor questioned. She just did it!

It amazes me that although my roommate was asleep, she inclined her ear to faith and pressed forward without regard to her flesh. And it was from this incident I realized that as an intercessor, you'll often be required to come outside of your comfort zone and push past your emotions and feelings.

Indeed, God is looking for a generation of intercessors who will remove self-inflicting constraints and rest on His Spirit. God's most precious gift is intercession, so much so that Jesus, "who is even at the right hand of God, *is assigned to* makes intercession for us Romans 8:34." Likewise, we, as believers, are called to intercede to a degree and magnitude according to our faith.

But, having faith is not only for those praying. The faith you apply in intercession is the same faith employed for receiving. In my case, because I had faith to look past my sleeping roommate, I received a divine breakthrough.

Today, I believe many are missing out on their blessings due to their lack of faith. We must look past all elements and look at God's heart concerning our situation.

For instance, when Samuel was looking for the next king to replace Saul, God's instructions explicitly stated not to look at the appearance, because God sees differently from man. He looks at our hearts.

Your heart and your faith are what moves God. As we stated in an earlier chapter, your faith is the currency of Heaven, and a heart posture that bears God's heartbeat is what causes mountains to move.

Yes, we must have faith and belief that God will move on our behalf. However, *though our faith game may be strong*, our heart posture is what vouches for us. The purity and sincerity of a heart that is poured out at Jesus' feet are what God is considering. He's looking for a pure and ready vessel whom He can work through.

So, it's when you bear the heartbeat of Jesus and boldly walk in faith that your ears become more fine-tuned to what the Spirit of the Lord is saying.

As an intercessor, you stand in the gap. You pray on behalf of someone or something. Therefore, your spirit must be sensitive to the move and callings of God. You must be able to hear rightly from God. It's crucial that as you pray, you're praying God's will and not the flesh nor the will of men.

Anna from the Old Testament is someone who knew the importance of praying from a heart posture that pleased God.

## Posture Right

Anna was a prophetic intercessor who was an elderly widow that was well into her late hundreds. She devoted her entire life to praying, fasting, and interceding on behalf of the birth and arrival and ministry of our Sweet King, Jesus.

Anna knew the scriptures and placed her faith in the Word of God. She knew the importance of looking beyond the faces and verdicts of men.

Anna was wise enough to know that her current circumstances (such as widowhood and old age) should not delimit the gifts and callings that God placed on her life. She prevailed and defied all odds. She constantly prayed and testified of Jesus until she eventually witnessed the breakthrough of her intercession.

Like Anna, we must understand that it is our job to pray until something happens. It's our God-given mandate to watch over our prayers. We must persist in faith, believing that as an ambassador of Christ, He hears our call and is actively working alongside us to shift and move our mountains.

However, the job of an intercessor isn't a stroll in the park but a serious business. Bearing God's heartbeat is nothing that should be taken lightly. Though it's a rewarding call, you must remain in the proper position and carefully watch to see what He will say to you.

And you might ask, what is the price of being an intercessor? Well, an intercessor is set apart for the Lord. An intercessor, bears God's heart and glory, in spirit and in truth, in purity, faith, and integrity. We must understand that we sustain a lifestyle of fasting, praying, and submitting our will to the Father so that we can pursue His will.

In truth, an intercessor is someone who's continuously consulting the ways of the Lord. They never intend on pleasing men. Instead, their focus and desires are to please God and win His heart.

Also, an intercessor's priority is the development and manifestation of the Kingdom of Heaven on earth. They care about the hearts and souls of men. And their desire is to see others live a life that is devoted to Christ.

Therefore, as an intercessor, you must abhor all that is evil; in fact, you stand in the front line combating the enemy as he tries to defy God's children. Your job as in intercessor is to properly align your heart, mind, and spirit with the Father's. You must understand that proper alignment is vital for ushering in His will and a breakthrough for His people.

### *You move God's Heart*

A few years ago, I was invited to a single mom's ministry. Though I'm not a single mom, nor was I a mother for that matter, I went. My intentions were to support the friend who invited me. I had no intention of ministering in any capacity.

But while I was there, there was a lady who broke down and needed someone to minister to her. At that moment, I looked at my friend, expecting her to step forward. I mean, she was the leader and curator after all.

For a moment, we sat there in a staring match, expecting the other to move. Suddenly, I realized my purpose for being there that night and thought, "seriously God?" I figured I was coasting for the night.'

The biggest mistake an intercessor or a child of God can make is to think that God is going to allow you 'coast' while there are gifts and talents that are within you. We must always be ready to move with God, both in season and out of season.

Shortly after, I began ministering. I read scriptures, prayed over the lady, and bound and rebuked all tormenting thoughts and spirits.

However, as we were leaving, a mocking spirit appeared and continued to antagonize her by saying, '*I didn't feel anything, it ain't work.*' For a split second, I questioned my authority, but thankfully God silenced my thoughts.

## Prayer Tool

During my ride home, the Lord led me to Mark 9:29 and told me to fast and pray during the weekend. My entire weekend consisted of binding, breaking, and rebuking everything that was not of God and losing the love and fullness of God over her life.

The following Sunday, before church, the lady ran to me, grabbed my hand, and placed it on her forehead. She said, *'I don't know what happened, but when I got home, I felt completely better. However, I need you to pray for me because my sinuses are acting up, and I have a headache'* MY LORD! The same woman who mocked my authority ran towards me for more healing.

I know that my obedience to the voice of God and my endurance to look past those manifesting spirits is what brought about her total restoration and healing. We must understand that though we pray and intercede, we must continue to apply the intensity of faith through fasting and praying.

On the other hand, we may not always record breakthroughs and changes. Yet, that doesn't mean that God isn't working. Our faith is the conduit, and God is always moving and working. Therefore, we must hold fast to our belief and trust that as an ambassador of Christ, we have the power to move mountains.

Meanwhile, after I prayed for the woman, there was a man who was limping. His limp seriously bothered me, so I called him and instantly prayed over his leg. Afterward, he looked at me as if I grew a million heads, thanked me, and walked away without a limp.

My God! He was healed! Like the woman with the jars of oil, the oil of the Lord continued to flow as I prayed for many others who came for service.

The truth is, when the Lord is ever moving in your life and on your behalf, you must be cautious about hindering the flow of the Holy Spirit.

1 Thessalonians 5:19 tells us not to quench the Holy Spirit. There are great and numerous things that God wants to do through His children. However, we must be intentional about understanding the move of God and allowing Him to move as He will.

We must look past our agendas and consider what the Holy Spirit wishes to do in our lives. It's in moving past our orders and customs that we make room for the flow of the Holy Spirit to surpass our understanding.

## Moving past your customs

2 Kings 4 highlights a woman who just became a single mother because her husband had kicked the bucket. This woman's husband was the breadwinner of the family and left them in debt, so she didn't have funds to pay her creditors.

As a result of this, she was in jeopardy of losing everything. Through her desperation, she cried out for help. Prophet Elisha stretched her faith and instructed her to sell all that she had so that she could make ends meet. The woman humbly said she only had a jar of old oil. Elisha then instructed her to borrow tons of vessels, so that she could ration out her oil and sell it.

The lady did what was instructed, and God miraculously increased her oil. Now, with each passing vessel, the oil of the Lord continued to flow. Once the last vessel was brought forth, the oil suddenly stopped flowing. One jar of oil turned into many filled vessels. The woman had an overwhelming abundance of oil. And once she sold her jars, she got out of debt and sustained herself with the leftovers.

When we move past our traditions, norms, and thinking, we pave the way for the Lord's exceedingly great move. For God's thoughts are not our thoughts, nor are our ways, His ways $_{\text{Isaiah 55:8}}$ and His works far exceeds ours.

Elisha knew the power of a faithful widow's mite. He knew that as he charged her with faith even over her last, God will excel her expectations.

Often, God charges us over our little. He watches our heart posture to determine if we'll remain faithful even amidst apparent lack. In the hands of God, little is more than enough. That's why God was able to exceedingly and abundantly move with the woman's oil and even with the simplicity of my roommate's prayer.

The truth is, whether or not you're called to the role of an 'intercessor' or 'prayer warrior,' God still moves and excels through your lack. Therefore, you may not always have the full language for your prayer request, but the Spirit does. Your act of faith is what moves God.

## *Without Language*

I once suffered from a severe case of eczema. One day after tending to my skincare needs, I became overwhelmingly engulfed with an uncontrollable itch. I tried everything, from showers to soothing creams, yet, there was absolutely nothing that would ease my pain. Out of desperation, I cried out, 'GOD PLEASE!'

I felt utterly desperate and broken to the point that those were the only words I could fathom. I didn't have language for what I wanted, needed, nor for what I experienced, but my spirit did. Within a matter of seconds, I was immersed in a deep peace that surpassed my understanding. The itch and the pain vanished suddenly.

I had such a mind-blowing experience that night. Even when in pain, and agony, words without sound shake Heaven! Yes, you may not always have the perfect words to form your prayers, but the Spirit of the Lord hears your heart. And Jesus listens to your spirit as he makes intercession for you. Also, your breakthrough may not always appear as you think it should.

Your breakthrough may result from a simple prayer. You may even be required to persist through fasting and prayer or even give your last in faith. Perhaps, just maybe, your breakthrough may come through words without sound. Indeed, an intercessor is one that pours out their heart to receive the fullness of the Lord.

And, as you arise to intercede on behalf of yourself and the needs of others, remember it's your faith and your heart posture that will create a breakthrough and change that's in partnership with Heaven.

Your prayer tool is a matter of your heart and your faith. You must trust in the Lord with all your heart and with all your might. You must believe that as you speak, God will move. You must understand that faith is voice-activated, so as you declare a thing, watch, for it will be established for you Job 12:28.

Notwithstanding, I urge you to remain in close connection and alignment with the Father, for life and death are in the power of the tongue Proverbs 18:22. Out of the abundance of the heart, the mouth speaks Luke 6:45.

Therefore, for your prayers to evoke the heartbeat of God, you must have an intimate relationship with Jesus. The heart and prayers of someone who is focused on God's will are due to an understanding that God is our Father.

Also, you must understand that as a child of God, God loves you and wishes to build a relationship with you. And this is one more reason why God's children should actively engage in prayer. Prayer is the heavenly communication device that connects us to the Father. Prayers move the heartbeat of God!

## Prayer Tool

*Prayer to increase your intercession*

Lord God, in Jesus' name, I thank You. Father, You're an awesome God. You are a relational Father, and You desire the hearts of Your children.

Father, I thank You for forgiving me and cleansing me like snow. In Jesus' name, I ask that You endue me with the spirit of prayer.

Father, I ask that You strengthen my heart, mind, and spirit to pray and intercede as You see fit. I desire to walk with You as You bring Heaven here on earth. Therefore, purify my heart and mind and ready my spirit.

Father, I thank You for showing me that prayer is more than words. Prayer is a heart exchange, while my faith is my currency.

Father, I thank You for this day, I shall intercede on behalf of my family, my life, and my friends.

Father, in Jesus' name, I will partner with Heaven as Christ's ambassador, and proudly I stand firm in the faith. Lord God, in Jesus' name, I thank You for the gift of faith and prayer. Amen.

# Prayer Tool Index

# Prayer Tool Index

50+ divinely inspired prayers for all your needs

## *Prayer Tool Index*

Prayer and Praise ................................................................... 128
Prayer for Abstinence ........................................................... 128
Prayer for Barren Women ..................................................... 129
Prayer for Breaking Spiritual Soul-ties ................................ 129
Prayer for Breakthrough with Fasting ................................. 130
Prayer for Breakthrough with Prayer .................................. 131
Prayer for Business Success .................................................. 131
Prayer for Children ................................................................ 132
Prayer for Church Impact ..................................................... 133
Prayer for Endurance ............................................................ 134
Prayer for Eyesight ................................................................ 134
Prayer for Faithfulness .......................................................... 135
Prayer for Family Unity ........................................................ 135
Prayer for Financial Breakthrough ...................................... 135
Prayer for Forgiveness .......................................................... 136
Prayer for Freedom from Alcohol Abuse ............................ 136
Prayer for Freedom from Anxiety ....................................... 137
Prayer for Freedom from Depression .................................. 137
Prayer for Freedom from Drug Abuse ................................ 138
Prayer for Freedom from Fear .............................................. 138
Prayer for Freedom from Suicidal Thoughts ...................... 139
Prayer for Future Spouse ...................................................... 140
Prayer for Gentleness ............................................................ 140
Prayer for Gifts and Callings ................................................ 141
Prayer for Godly Friends ...................................................... 141
Prayer for Goodness .............................................................. 142
Prayer for Healing of Spine .................................................. 142
Prayer for Heart Health ........................................................ 143
Prayer for Heartbreak ............................................................ 143
Prayer for Intimacy with God .............................................. 144
Prayer for Joy ......................................................................... 144
Prayer for Kindness ............................................................... 145
Prayer for Kingdom Relationship ........................................ 145

Prayer for Knee Relief ..................................................................... 146
Prayer for Longsuffering .................................................................. 146
Prayer for Loved One's Health ....................................................... 147
Prayer for Loved One's Salvation .................................................. 147
Prayer for Marriage Restoration .................................................... 148
Prayer for Men's Health .................................................................. 148
Prayer for Mental Health ................................................................. 149
Prayer for Ministry Impact .............................................................. 149
Prayer for Nonprofit Impact ............................................................ 150
Prayer for Peace ............................................................................... 150
Prayer for Persecuted Church ........................................................ 150
Prayer for Personal Health ............................................................. 151
Prayer for Physical Healing ............................................................ 151
Prayer for Purity Sustainability ...................................................... 152
Prayer for Restful night .................................................................. 152
Prayer for Safety .............................................................................. 152
Prayer for Schooling ....................................................................... 153
Prayer for Self-control .................................................................... 154
Prayer for Sharing the Gospel ....................................................... 154
Prayer for Spiritual Armor .............................................................. 155
Prayer for Spiritual Healing ........................................................... 156
Prayer for Spiritual Sight ................................................................ 156
Prayer for Understanding ............................................................... 157
Prayer for Wealth ............................................................................. 157
Prayer for Wisdom ........................................................................... 157
Prayer for Women's Health ............................................................ 158

*Prayer Tool Index*

## Prayer Tool Index

### Prayer and Praise

Father, You are worthy. Lord, I praise You. Father, I love You. Lord, I thank You. Your hands alone created the Heavens and the earth. By Your Words, we were formed. Lord, without You, nothing is made that was made. Father, I thank You for calling me Your own and for choosing me as Your child. Lord, I love You, and I thank You.

Father, I thank You for Your sweet Son, Precious Jesus. Lord, thank You for His Blood. Oh God! His Blood has purified me and washed me clean. Lord, thank You for sending Your comforting Spirit, Your Holy Spirit. For by Your Spirit, I am guided, and I have communion with You. Father, thank You for You. In Your Son Jesus' name, I pray. Amen.

### Prayer for Abstinence

God, I bless Your name. Father, I honor You for You, oh God, are my Lord. Heavenly Father, I know You are King of kings and Lord of Lords. Oh, Father! How You desire to see all Your creations honor You in spirit and in truth.

So, Father, I repent for dishonoring You with my life. Lord, I ask that You sustain me as I present my body and life before You. For Lord, Your Words in Romans 12:1 says that I should present my body as a living sacrifice, holy and acceptable to You because it is my reasonable service. So, Father, in Jesus' name, I ask that You send Your Holy

Spirit. To guide me, protect me, and convict me as I walk my journey of honoring You, physically, emotionally, and mentally.

Lord, I desire to walk pure before You so Father, I ask that You restore my purity and make me whole. In Jesus' name, I pray, amen.

### *Prayer for Barren Women*

Lord, I bless your name as I pour my heart to You. Father, as a woman who hungers for children. Lord, I pour my tears at Your feet, and I ask that You have mercy on me. Lord, You're the author of healing and miraculous breakthrough so, Father I ask that You heal and open my womb in Jesus' name. Father, for Your glory, by faith, I stand in agreement that as You bless me with a child, I will commit my baby back to You.

Father, in Jesus' name, by faith, I thank You for opening my womb, and cleaning me so that I can bring forth a healthy and whole child. In Jesus' name, I pray, amen.

### *Prayer for Breaking Spiritual Soul-ties*

Lord God, You alone are holy. Father, You alone are worthy. Lord, I repent of all known and unknown sins. Lord, I forgive all who've hurt me. Father, in Jesus' name, I ask that You reveal Your sovereign will over my life.

Lord, I'm also praying that You bind and rebuke every demonic spirit that is working within and around me. Father, I ask that You purify my soul of all soul ties. Lord, in Jesus' name, I bind, break, and rebuke everything that is operating within and around me that is not sent by You. Father, by the Blood of Jesus' I declare freedom over my life.

By the Blood of Jesus, I break the power of witchcraft. By the Blood of Jesus, I break the power of all ungodly ties. By the Blood of Jesus, I am wash cleaned and made new. In Jesus' name, I loose Your peace over my life. I loose wholeness and purity within my soul. In Jesus' name, I declare that every chain and hindrance is broken. I decree that I am set free and walking in victory. Father, I declare that Your perfect love abounds within me. So, Father, I loose Your anointing and power over my life. In Jesus' name, I pray, amen.

### Prayer for Breakthrough with Fasting

Lord God, Your Word says that You've designated fasting to break yokes and to set the captives free. Lord, I also know that such fast as you have commanded builds my relationship with You. So, Father, I ask for Your strategic wisdom and understanding as it pertains to fasting.

Lord, I pray that through obedience and endurance, my fasting is most pleasing and made holy unto You. Lord God, I thank You for building Your Spirit of longsuffering within me. Father, I ask that You increase my understanding concerning Your will and Your way. Oh God! Thank You for ordering my steps within Your Word. In Jesus' name, I pray, amen.

## Prayer for Breakthrough with Prayer

Oh God, You are a wondrous God! Father, the heavens and earth bow down before You. All of eternity worships Your name. Father, I thank You for purifying my heart and mind. Father, I thank You for putting words in my mouth. Lord, I thank You for establishing the heart of prayer within me. Lord, I thank You that You hear me when I call to You.

Heavenly Father, I thank You that You desire to commune with me. Father, You call me Your own, and You said Your sheep knows Your Voice. So, Father, I thank You for fine-tuning my ears and understanding so that I can perceive You. And Father, I thank You for establishing Your will within my heart.

Lord, as I pray, change happens. When I pray, the breakthrough is evident. Lord, when I pray, lives are saved for Your namesake. Lord, when I pray, I pray Your will and Your heart. So, Father, I thank You for establishing Your will and love within me, Father I thank You, for by Your Words You are creating me to pray an effectual fervent prayer. In Your Son, Jesus' name, I pray, amen.

## Prayer for Business Success

Father, You are glorious. Lord, You are holy. Lord, You are worthy. You desire to see nations honor You. Father, I ask That You circumcise my heart so that in all my ways, I please You. Lord God, I ask that as I continue in business, I ask that You blow Your breath in everything

I do. Lord, I decree that I'm blessed with more clientele, more income, more innovative ideas. Father, I even ask that You grant me wisdom on how to share Your love and testimony even within my place of business. Holy Spirit, I ask that You cover me as I live a life of integrity, honesty, and godly ethical standard. Lord, in all my ways, I desire to be set apart and represent You to the highest degree. In Your Son, Sweet Jesus' name, I pray, amen.

### *Prayer for Children*

*Train up a child in the way he should go, and when he is old, he will not depart from it. – Proverbs 22:6*

Oh Lord, In Jesus' name, Father, I thank You for gifting me with children. Father, I ask for wisdom and understanding as I teach, love, and raise the child(ren) You've blessed me with. Father, I ask that You watch over my child(ren) all the days of their lives. Father, I ask that Your spirit resides in them, and You keep them in Your arms. Father, I pray that they'll forever know Your voice and know Your love. Lord, I ask that they grow in love and forgiveness as they watch my faults and learn from my shortcomings.

Father, I thank You for giving my child(ren) understanding and love as they understand that we are in a sin-filled world, and all have sinned and fallen short of Your glory. Lord, in Jesus' name, I thank You for placing a hedge of protection around my child and for blessing them more than I can imagine. In Your precious Son, Jesus' name, I pray, amen.

### *Prayer for Church Impact*

Father, thank You for blessing Your children with a church body that can impact nations with Your great love. Father, I ask that You bless every congregation from the pulpits to the pews. Lord, in Jesus' name, I bind and rebuke the spirit of lethargy, weariness, strife, and unforgiveness. Lord, God, I loose Your perfect love, Your perfect strength, and Your perfect understanding in Jesus' name.

Lord God, I thank You that the Body of Christ, knows the importance of understanding, unity, and love. Father, I thank You that within our church body, we have a solid foundation of Your true Word. Father, in Jesus' name, I loose an abundance of signs, wonders, gifts, and miraculous miracles.

Heavenly Father. I stand in agreement with other members that Your church body is healed, whole, and delivered in Jesus' name. Father, I stand in agreement that every staff and every member knows how to have an intimate and personal relationship with You. Lord, I thank You that Your church influence and love exudes beyond any four walls. Lord, I thank You for a loving community that knows how to honor and love Your Word and will. In Jesus' name, I pray, amen.

*Prayer Tool Index*

## *Prayer for Endurance*

Thank You, Holy Spirit, for Your strength. Thank You, Lord, for Your power. For by You, I can stand. Lord, by Your love, I can walk by faith and not by sight. Father, by Your Spirit, You give me power when I'm weak and Lord, You increase my strength. Father, I thank You for allowing me to wait on You as You renew my strength.

Father, because You've shown me how to endure and how to stand, I can mount up on with wings like eagles. Father, I can now run and not be weary. So, Father, thank You, for I will walk and not faint. Lord, my God, thank You for Your Spirit of endurance. For by You I can do all things as You strengthen me. In Jesus' name, I pray, amen.

## *Prayer for Eyesight*

Lord God, You alone can do all things. Father, I thank You for Your unmatched healing anointing. Lord, thank You for clear vision in Jesus' name. Lord, thank You for healing and restoring my eyesight. Father, thank You for by faith, I believe that both my spiritual sight and my physical sight is enhanced. Thank You, Lord, for now, I can see Your will clearly. Lord, I'm confident that You've established my vision in Your truth and Your will. So, Father, thank You for healing, restoration, and clarity. In Your Son Jesus' name, I pray, amen.

## Prayer for Faithfulness

God, I thank You for Your Spirit of conviction. Lord, I thank You for leading me in the path of righteousness and a path that is most pleasing to You. Father, in Jesus' name, I ask that You increase my faith, and create in me a noble spirit. Father, You are glorious, and You desire a faithful servant. So, Lord, thank You for showing me how to be faithful in all my ways. In Jesus' name, I pray, amen.

## Prayer for Family Unity

Father, by faith, I declare and decree that my house will honor You. Father, I decree that every familial divisiveness is broken in the name of Jesus. Lord, I pray for family unity and love. Lord, I pray that my entire lineage is blessed by Your name. Father, I plead the blood of Jesus throughout my entire bloodline. I decree family healing, family wholeness, and family unification by the Blood of the Lamb. So, Father, I thank You for cleansing my family for Your namesake. In Jesus' name, I thank You, amen.

## Prayer for Financial Breakthrough

Father, I thank You for breaking generational curses from my life and my family's lineage. Oh God, I thank You for generational victories. Lord, I praise Your name for You have shown me how to steward my finances according to Your Kingdom. Father, You have blessed me with self-control, Oh Lord, for now, I no longer spend or make decisions from impulse. Father, I am wise in my actions and my spending. Lord God, thank You for strategic and innovative ideas where I can generate wealth and abundance for my family and me.

Lord, I thank You for showing me the blessing of being able to give back to Your Kingdom. Oh God, I thank You for all Your blessings according to Your riches in glory. Father, in Jesus' name I pray, amen.

## *Prayer for Forgiveness*

Father, in Jesus' name, I thank You for the Balm that You've placed in my midst. Lord, I ask that Your perfect time continues to heal my heart and the heart of those I've offended and those who have hurt me. In Jesus' name, I decree that the burden and weight of unforgiveness shall no longer bound me. Lord, In Jesus' name, I ask that You release the burden of unforgiveness of those who are carrying it towards me.

In Jesus' name, I thank you for purifying my heart and mind. Lord, I ask for grace and provision as You walk me through the process of forgiving myself and my offenders. Lord, I also ask that You bring a wave of healing to myself and for those whom I have offended. Father, thank You for the Spirit of forgiveness. In Jesus' name, I pray, amen.

## *Prayer for Freedom from Alcohol Abuse*

Father, in Jesus' name Lord I thank You for Your restorative anointing. Lord, I thank You for Your Fatherly embrace. God, I thank You for Your spirit of honesty and Your revelation. Lord, God, thank You for Your Spirit of endurance. Father, I thank You for filling my every void.

Father, In Jesus' name, I thank You for breaking off the spirit of drunkenness and alcoholism. Lord God, in Jesus' name, thank You for walking me in Your freedom and victory over alcohol abuse. In Jesus' name, I pray, amen.

## *Prayer for Freedom from Anxiety*

Lord God, I thank You for Jesus' peace that surpasses all my understanding. Father, I thank You for Your comforting and calming Spirit. Father, I thank You for allowing me to cast all my cares on You.

Oh Lord, thank You for showing me that You care for me. In Jesus' name, I am free from all anxiety attacks. Lord, in You, I am healed and whole. Father, thank You, for You are my provider. Father, thank You, for You are my sustainer. Father, thank You, for You are my peace. Father, thank You for being all things for me. In Your precious Son's name, I pray, amen.

## *Prayer for Freedom from Depression*

Father, I thank You for Your joy and Your peace. Lord, I thank You for tearing the veil from my eyes, and now I see that I am not alone. Father, thank You for being my Father. Thank You for loving me. Lord, thank You for my family and my friends. Father, thank You for creating the spirit of freedom within me. Lord, thank You for planting Your seeds of Love within me.

Father, thank You for I walk differently because I am no longer bound by depression; neither am I bound by depressive thoughts. Lord, thank You for giving me wisdom and understanding. For by Your truth, I am mindful of what thoughts I allow in my mind. Father, thank You, Lord, I understand that my body is Your temple, and You desire me. Lord God, in Jesus' name, father, I thank You for Freedom. Amen.

## *Prayer for Freedom from Drug Abuse*

Hallelujah Jesus! I declare that I am free. Lord, I decree that I am no longer bound. I walk freely as I receive my blessings and victory. I thank You for breaking the power of addiction from my life. Lord, I thank You for breaking the power of habitual bad habits and wrong decision making.

Lord, God, I thank You for divine understanding and a desire for the life that You've given me. Father, I thank You for healing and restoration. I thank You for filling every void. Oh God, I thank You for giving me a desire for all things that concerns You. Lord, I thank You for freedom and victory. In Jesus' name, I pray, amen.

## *Prayer for Freedom from Fear*

1 John 4:8-9 *"for God is love. In this, the love of God was manifested toward us, that God has sent His only begotten Son into the world, that we might live through Him."*

1 John 4:18 *"There is no fear in love; but perfect love casts out fear."*

Father, I thank You for being LOVE. I thank You for endowing me in Your love. And I thank You that, in You, I rest in love. For Father, in You, I am complete and lacking nothing. Oh God, I thank You that there is no fear in me for Father; you said if I abide in You, then You'll abide in Me. Oh Lord, You have said You are love, and there is no fear in love, for Your perfect love has cast out all fear. Father, thank You for the sweet revelation of the magnitude of Your love. Father, thank You for filling me with Your Love. Holy Spirit, thank You for keeping my feet from fear and for planting me in Your bosom. Father, in Jesus' name, I thank You for Your abundance. In Jesus' name, I pray, amen.

### *Prayer for Freedom from Suicidal Thoughts*

Father, I thank You for life and life more abundantly. Lord God, I thank You for the Blood of Jesus that runs through my veins. Father, I thank You for tearing the blinding veil from my eyes.

Lord, I thank You for showing me that I am valuable, loved, and wanted. Father, I thank You for the desire to live. Father, I thank You that I now know and understand that I am not a mistake, nor am I forgotten. Lord, I thank You for Your comforting Spirit and warm embrace. God, I love You, and I love the life that You've given me.

Father, God, I thank You for sound counsel and encouraging friends and family members. Lord, I thank You for my community, who are invested in me and have my best interest in mind. Lord, I thank You for Your wisdom and understanding in all things. In Your Son, Jesus' name, I pray, amen.

### *Prayer for Future Spouse*

Lord God, I thank You for building me and crafting me in Your image. Father, I ask that during this season of waiting, that You continue to prepare me and build me for Your namesake. Lord, mold me how You see fit. Father, purify my heart of all things that are not of You. Father, create in me a new image concerning Your love and my value in Your eyes.

Father, I know that it is not good for man to be alone, so Lord, I ask that You bring forth the helper that is compatible with me. Father, I pray that I grow to love my companion as Christ loves us. I ask that I am ready to be the spouse that my helper deserves. And Lord, I pray that my spouse is the person whom I need. Lord, I ask that we learn the true meaning and value of love as we love each other. Father, I ask that in Your perfect timing, allow us to draw near and meet knowing that we were made for one another.

Lord, I thank You for creating a husband/wife that is a companion for me. In Your Son Jesus' name, I pray, amen.

### *Prayer for Gentleness*

Father, I thank You for Your sweet and gentle Spirit. Lord, I thank You for showing me how to be meek and gentle as a lamb but as bold as a lion. Father, I thank You for showing me how to love others as You would see fit. Lord, I thank You for allowing me to walk with a spirit of peace, gentleness, and love. Lord, I thank You that I am not easily frazzled, nor is my countenance easily thrown off. Father, I thank You for the authority that comes from a gentle and quiet spirit. Father, I thank You for the peace of Jesus. In Jesus' name, I pray, amen.

## *Prayer for Gifts and Callings*

Father, in Jesus' name, I ask that You stir up the gifts and callings that are within me. Lord, I ask that You show me how to honor You with my life. Father, I ask that You plant and cultivate Your love and fruit of the Spirit within me so that as I flourish in my gifts and callings, I'll always honor You and love You. Father, I ask that You develop my character, my mentality, and my spirit.

Father, I ask that You prune away everything that is not of You. Father, I ask that You wash me clean and fill me with Your Spirit. Lord, God, I desire to be used by You. So, Father, here I am, use me as You please. Stir me for Your glory, and position me for Your Kingdom. In Your Son Jesus' name, I pray, amen.

## *Prayer for Godly Friends*

Father, I thank You that You've mended my heart and mind to be able to receive companionship in the form of friends. Father, I thank You that You saw fit that I am never alone.

Father, I thank You for showing me how to love my friends and how to be friendly. Father, I thank You that You're placing like-minded individuals in my corner who will love, support, and encourage me. Father, I thank You for a group of friends where we can love on You and magnify Your name. Father, I thank You for the uniqueness within my tribe and community. I thank You for binding jealousy, envy, and strife. Lord, I thank You for setting loose love, compassion, and understanding. Lord, I declare that all my relationships will honor and glorify You. Father, I thank You for what You are doing in this time and in this hour. In Your Son Jesus' name, I pray, amen.

### *Prayer for Goodness*

Lord, You are good, and I thank You for Your goodness. Lord, I thank You that Your goodness flows through me. Lord, I thank You that I have the desire to do good to all men. Father, I thank You that You've given me charge to walk in Your Spirit of ethics. Father, I thank You for entrusting me with Your integrity. Father, in Jesus' name, I thank You for allowing me to bear the heartbeat of Jesus. Father, You're an amazing and a good Father. I thank You for showing me Your goodness so that I too may walk in it. In Jesus' name, I pray, amen.

### *Prayer for Healing of Spine*

Father, You are Jehovah Rapha, Lord You are my healer. Father, I believe only by Your hands, You can heal. Lord, I ask that You place the palm of Your hands on my back. Father, strengthen my spine.

Lubricate my joints and expand my body's elasticity. Lord, I ask that You heal every aching bone and ailment that is within my body and, more specifically, of my spine. Father, I know You can miraculously heal me. So, Father, I trust that You will. In Jesus' name, I pray, amen.

### *Prayer for Heartbreak*

Father, You are HEALER. Lord, I thank You for mending my soul and for restoring my mind. Father, I thank You for allowing me to sit at Your feet as You reveal Your love to me. Father, I thank You that Your love has never changed. Father, I thank You that You call me beloved and that You care earnestly for me. Father, I thank You that You're still showing me how to love with care and compassion, even after this heartbreak.

Father, I thank You for Your Spirit of forgiveness, for by Your forgiveness, I can fully heal. Lord, I am ready for You to continue to pour Your oil on me. Father, I thank You because you care for me. In Jesus' name, I pray, amen.

### *Prayer for Heart Health*

Father, God, In Jesus' name, I thank You for outlining my dietary needs and exercise regimen. Lord, I thank You for establishing Your heart within mine. Father, I have faith that You know my ending from the beginning. Lord, I trust that my entire life is in Your hands. Therefore, I commit my heart and the doctor's reports into Your hands. Father, I choose to believe Your report. Father, I believe You will heal and restore my heart, Father, in faith, I stand in agreement and receive my full healing. Father in Jesus' name, I ask that if I am holding onto unbelief, doubt, and unforgiveness, Lord I ask that You reveal it, and purge it from my heart and mind. Father, I thank You that I can receive my healing in peace. In Your Son Jesus' name, Lord, I thank You. Amen.

### *Prayer for Intimacy with God*

Father, You are a loving God. Father, You are the true Lord who desires Your children. Father, I thank You that as the Creator of all, You still desire me. Lord, I thank You that as a Father, You are calling me closer to You. Father, even while I was still in my sins and trespasses, Oh Lord, You desired me. So, Father, as You're calling me, I am drawing closer. Father, continue to pull me closer to You. Father, continue to show me a deeper level of Your love and intimacy. Father, I ask that You show me the fullness of Your heart and the fullness of Your love. Father, I thank You for allowing me to commune at Your feet. For in Your presence is where I desire to be. Father, in Jesus' name, I thank You for Your sweet communion. Amen.

### *Prayer for Joy*

Lord God, I thank You for a merriness that could never be robbed. Father, I thank You for pure joy. Oh Lord, I thank You for turning my mourning into laughter. Father, I thank You for turning my sorrows into gladness. Father, I thank You that in all things, I can find my joy in You. Oh God, I thank You that in all things I can look towards You. Lord, I thank You for contagious JOY! Father, I thank You that my joy spreads throughout the nations. Lord, I thank You for showing me how to find joy and peace throughout all seasons of life. Father, You are a glorious Father, and Lord, I thank You. Amen.

## *Prayer for Kindness*

Father, You are a loving and kind Father. Lord, I thank You for showing me how to rest in You. Lord, I thank You for showing me how to cast out doubt and rage. Father, I thank You for pure kindness and love. Lord, I desire to know more of Your kindness, so Father, in Jesus' name, I ask that You endow me with Your kindness so that I may edify others with Your love. Lord, in Jesus' name, I thank You for Your grace. Amen.

## *Prayer for Kingdom Relationship*

Father, I thank You that You alone open and shut doors. Father, I thank You that the doors You've shut can never be opened by man. And Lord, I thank You that the doors You've opened can never be shut by man. So, Father, I ask that You position me to receive all that You have for my life.

Lord, I ask that You align and order my steps for Your glory. Father, I thank You for all the Kingdom relationships that are forming. Father,

I ask that You prepare me mentally and spiritually so that I can adequately steward over Your gifts. Lord, I ask that You prepare the hearts and minds of those whom You've called to receive me. Likewise, prepare my heart and mind as I receive those whom You've called me to. Father, I thank You for strategic divine alignment for Your glory. In Jesus' name, I bless You. Amen.

### *Prayer for Knee Relief*

Father, in Jesus' name, I declare that every joint in my body come into alignment right NOW! Father, I urge every bone and ligament functioning within my knee and legs, to align: bone to bone, joint to joint. Lord God, in Jesus' name, I declare that every swelling and inflammation is gone in the name of Jesus. Father, as I place my hands on my knee, I declare Your fire to bring forth healing supernaturally. Father, as I stand in faith, I proclaim Your greatness, for You alone bring healing. So, Father, in Jesus' name, I thank You for my perfect health and perfect posture. In Jesus' name, amen.

### *Prayer for Longsuffering*

Oh God, I thank You for Your Spirit of perseverance. Father, I thank You for pruning me and for molding me. I thank You for creating in me a righteous spirit. Father, I thank You for allowing Your spirit to rest on me so that I may endure in You.

Father, I thank You because no weapon formed against me shall prosper. Oh Lord, You have blessed me in all my ways. So, Father, thank You for Your Spirit and for Your might. In Your precious Son Jesus', name I pray, amen.

## *Prayer for Loved One's Health*

Father, in Jesus' name, I thank You for the spirit and gift of intercession. Lord God, I thank You for working and moving by faith. Father in Jesus' name I call out _____ (name of loved one(s)) and declare supernatural and divine healing. Father, I thank You for covering over _____ in the Blood of Jesus. Lord, I speak forth Your perfect will and peace over _____. In Jesus' name, I thank You. Amen.

## *Prayer for Loved One's Salvation*

Father in Jesus' name I call forth _____ (name of loved one(s). Lord, I stand in the gap and declare that they will know and love You in Jesus' name. Father, I decree that _____ is Your child. Father, I ask that You do a complete work on their heart and mind. Father, I thank You for placing Your eyes on _____. Lord God, I declare that their entire house is blessed and filled with Your love and presence. Father, in Jesus' name, I thank You because You hear my heart-cry. Amen.

## Prayer Tool Index

### Prayer for Marriage Restoration

Father, I thank You for the gift and love of marriage. Lord God, in Jesus' name, I ask that You reveal every attack from the enemy and condemn it to a thing of not. Father, I ask that You repair our love and restore our marriage for Your glory. Father, in Jesus' name, I declare an abundance of peace within my heart and marriage. Lord God, I thank You for a marriage that is an example of the Love of Christ. Father, I thank You that our marriage is an example of hope, healing, and faith for others. Father, in Jesus' name, I ask that Your will be done. In Jesus' name, Father, I thank You, amen.

### Prayer for Men's Health

Father, in Jesus' name, I declare complete and total healing within the men's reproductive system. Father, I decree that my testosterone and all other hormones function correctly in the name of Jesus. Father, I bind every spirit that is interfering with my manly health in Jesus' name. Father, I loose Your perfect healing and love. Father, I decree that my entire body is blessed. Father, I decree that I am in complete alignment with Your words.

Father, in Jesus' name, thank You for showing me how to properly tend to the temple You've given me. Lord God, in Jesus' name, I thank You for Your sovereign healing, sovereign peace, and sovereign wisdom. In Jesus' name, I thank You for my Manly health. Amen.

## Prayer for Mental Health

Father, in Jesus' name, I declare and decree mental health that is responsive and in full alignment with Your word. Father, I declare the peace of Heaven to surpass all understanding. Father, in Jesus' name, I thank You for a sound and righteous mind. Father, I thank You for keeping me in all my ways. Lord God, I declare that understanding and wisdom is my portion. In Jesus' name, I pray, amen.

## Prayer for Ministry Impact

Father, in Jesus' name, I thank You for blessing me with the gift of ministry. Father, I thank You for binding emotions, confusion, and doubt. Lord, God, I loose Your perfect love, wisdom, and understanding. Father, I thank You for granting me the tools and love to deliver Your ministry and message in the fashion in which You see fit. Father, in Jesus' name, I declare that the ministry You've blessed me with is for Your glory. Father, I decree that every member that encounters Your ministry is transformed in Your image.

Lord God, in Jesus' name, I thank You for the double portion. Father, I thank You for endowing me with more of Your wisdom, gifts and anointing to move as You lead. Father, I thank You for the proper support, volunteers, and finances. Lord God, in Jesus' name, have Your way. Amen.

## *Prayer Tool Index*

### *Prayer for Nonprofit Impact*

Father, in Jesus' name, Lord, God, I thank You for giving me the vision of service. Father, in Jesus' name, I decree that our nonprofit will flourish for Your glory. Father, I declare an impactful change as a result of our efforts. Father, in Jesus' name, I thank You for the perfect team and support. Father, in Jesus' name, I decree finances and divine provision to come forth. In Jesus' name, I pray, amen.

### *Prayer for Peace*

Father, in Jesus' name, I thank You for perfect peace. Lord God, I decree that I will no longer be swayed with the worries of this world. Father, I declare that my mind is fixed on Your love. Lord God, in Jesus' name, I thank You for showing me how to rest in You as You lead me in the path that You've set. Father, in Jesus' name, I decree that from this day forward, I shall walk in peace. I shall be an agent of peace. Father, in Jesus' name, I declare that peace shall be in my midst. In Jesus' name, I pray, amen.

### *Prayer for Persecuted Church*

Father, in Jesus' name, thank You for watching over Your servants. Lord God. I declare a hedge of safety over Your children. Father, in Jesus' name, I thank You that no weapon formed against Your children will prosper and every tongue that rises against Your seed shall be condemned. Lord God, I thank You for Your abundance of blessings. Father, I thank You for encouraging Your children. Lord

God, I thank You for giving Your children faith and strength to carry out the tasks that You've set before them. Oh God, bless Your children exceedingly and keep their feet in Your paths. In Jesus' name, I bless Your name. Amen.

## Prayer for Personal Health

Father God, Lord, I have many unmentionable needs. Lord, I ask that You place Your hands on my entire body, from the crown of my head to the soles of my feet. Father, in Jesus' name, I command my soul to come into full alignment with Your Word. Father, in Jesus' name, I believe that You can do great and marvelous works through my body. So, Father, I call You Healer as I call forth my healing. Lord, God, I thank You for full and total body restoration. In Jesus' name, I thank You. Amen.

## Prayer for Physical Healing

Lord, God, in Jesus' name, I thank You. Your eyes have seen, and Your ears have heard of the afflictions that are upon me, and you can feel them just as I can. Father, I ask that You heal me from the inside out. Lord God, I ask for wisdom on the proper diet that will help foster my healing. Lord God, I pray for strength as I stand in faith. Father, speak the Words, and I will do. Lord call it forth, and I am healed. Father, as the woman with the issue of blood, I will lift my hands in faith and expectation of healing. So, Father, I am assured that I will receive healing. Father, in Jesus' name, I thank You for my healing. Amen.

### Prayer for Purity Sustainability

Lord God, in Jesus' name. Father, I thank You for showing me how to honor You with my life and body. Father, I thank You for keeping the essence of my purity since birth. Father, in Jesus' name, I ask that You continue to keep my feet from being moved by the pleasures of this world.

Father, in Jesus' name, I thank You for allowing me to be a living and walking testimony for Your glory. Father, in Jesus' name, I thank You for Your blessing in keeping me. Lord, God, I ask that You continue to keep me for Your Glory. Father, in Jesus' name, I ask that in Your perfect time that You will send forth my spouse. In Jesus' name, Lord, I thank You. Amen.

### Prayer for Restful night

Father, in Jesus' name, Lord, I thank You for sweet and precious sleep. Father, I thank You that even at night, You've given my angels charge over me. Lord God, I thank You for allowing me to rest in Your bosom. Father, in Jesus' name, I thank You for allowing me to wake up fully rested and restored. In Jesus' name, I pray. Amen.

### Prayer for Safety

Father, I thank You that, as I dwell in Your secret place, I shall abide under Your shadow. Father, I will declare that You are my refuge and my fortress. My God, I will trust in You. Father, I have faith that You will deliver me from the snare of the fowler and from the perilous pestilence. Father, I know that as Your child, You shall cover me with Your feathers, and under Your wings, I shall take refuge.

Father, Your truth shall be my shield and buckler. Father, I declare that I shall not be afraid of the terror by night nor of the arrow that flies by day. Father, I will not fear the pestilence that walks in the darkness nor the destruction that lay waste at noonday. Lord, God, by the Blood of Jesus, I shall stand in Faith. For You alone are God, and in You, I shall trust. In Jesus' name I pray, amen. – Psalms 91:1-6

## *Prayer for Schooling*

Father, in Jesus' name, I ask that You place a hedge of protection around every individual and specifically those who are within of my household. Lord, I pray that You camp Your angels and give them the charge of protection to watch over them, tend to them and keep their feet from stumbling.

Father, in Jesus' name, I ask that You keep them as they travel to and from school. Lord, I ask that You grant me peace of mind, even with my schooling. Father, in Jesus' name, I ask that You cover this household with Your Spirit of excellence and grace. Father, I thank You that we are great stewards of knowledge and truth. Father, in Jesus' name, I thank You that we are honorable men and women for Your Kingdom.

## Prayer Tool Index

Lord, God in Jesus' I thank You for covering all school systems of every kind and every pupil, in Jesus' name. Thank You for Your great safety and provision. In Jesus' name, I pray, amen.

### Prayer for Self-control

Father, You honor Your great children who use wisdom to speak as You lead. Father, in Jesus' name, I ask for an overwhelming grace of self-control. Father, I ask that You strengthen my mind and heart as I walk with patience, peace, and endurance.

Father, I declare that I exercise self-control over my eating habits, over my tongue, over my heart, and over my emotions and thinking. Father, In Jesus' name, as I walk in self-control, I submit all my cares into Your hands. For Holy Father, Your Spirit alone brings wisdom, endurance, and self-control. So, Lord, I thank You for Your mighty hand as You lead me. In Your Son Jesus' name, I pray, amen.

### Prayer for Sharing the Gospel

Lord, God, I thank You that sharing Your love and Word does not require a title. Father, I thank You that we may all share Your love according to the grace and faith that works in us. Father, in Jesus' name, I ask that You endow me with Your words and with Your heart as I step out in faith, to share the great and best news of Jesus Christ. Lord, I declare that as I speak, I speak with clarity, truth, and understanding.

Lord God, in Jesus' name, I thank You for opening new doors and granting me excitement and wisdom to share Your Word and Love with those around me. Father, in Jesus' name, I thank You for Your Spirit and Your faithfulness. Amen.

## *Prayer for Spiritual Armor*

Lord, I am clothed in Your majesty. I am graced in Your armor. I am honored to bear Your sword. So, Father, I thank You for Your Spiritual Armor. Oh Lord, I will walk with Your integrity, love, and authority. Father, I thank You for the faith and wisdom to abhor what is not of You. Father, I thank You for the authority to cast down every imaginative thought that is contrary to Your Kingdom.

Father, I thank You for Your truth and wisdom to speak with Love and authority. Father, I thank You for spiritual eyesight to see spiritual things. Lord God, I thank You for Your authority to pull down, pluck out, remove, bind, and rebuke everything that is not of You. Father, I thank You for Your Spirit that allows me to call forth those things that are not as though they were. Father, I thank You for Your Words that You've planted in me to call forth Your Kingdom, to call forth Your love, and to call forth Your Truth. In Jesus' name, I thank You for Your Spiritual armor. Amen.

*Prayer Tool Index*

## *Prayer for Spiritual Healing*

Father, I rejoice that You see all my wounds. Lord, I thank You that You're tending to my every need. Father, even when it seems as if I'm not growing nor does it feel like I'm healing, Lord, I thank You because You are still moving. Father, I thank You, for Your truth and revelations. Lord, I thank You for allowing me to see that Your timing is perfect and that I am precious to You.

Therefore, Lord, You will spend as much time that is needed for my spiritual health and healing. Lord, God, in Jesus' name, I choose to partner with You for my healing. Therefore, I forgive myself and all my offenders. Father, I ask that You clear away every dirt and debris and fill my voids with Your love and truth. In Jesus' name, I plead the blood of Jesus over my life and heart. Amen.

## *Prayer for Spiritual Sight*

Father, in Jesus' name, I thank You, that I am Your child, for because of such, You have shown me the mysteries of the Kingdom of Heaven. Lord, in Jesus' name, I ask that You increase my portion according to my faith. Father, I ask that Your Holy Spirit guides me and nurtures my spirit as I learn more of the spiritual. Father, in Jesus' name, I thank You for enlarging my understanding as You expand my spiritual eyesight. In Jesus' name, I thank You. Amen.

### *Prayer for Understanding*

Father, I hunger and thirst for Your understanding. Father, in Jesus' name, be my Teacher and reveal to me, wise and marvelous things. Father enlarge my understanding. Lord God give me pure clarity to see and perceive things as You wish. Father, I ask that I walk with compassion and understanding. Lord, God, I thank You for endowing me with more of Your heavenly insight. In Jesus' name, I pray, amen.

### *Prayer for Wealth*

Father, I thank You that You have given Your children wisdom and understanding of Your wealth. Father, in Jesus' name, I ask that You increase me spiritually and physically with Your heavenly wealth. Father, God, I thank You that You've given me according to Your riches and glory. Father, I thank You that You have created me to be Your faithful steward. Father, thank You for showing me how to tend to the things that You have given me properly. Father, for Your glory, I shall give back to You and others. Father, for Your glory, I shall walk with a healthy spirit of wealth. In Jesus' name, I thank You. Amen.

### *Prayer for Wisdom*

Father, I thank You for wisdom. Lord, God, I declare that I have divine wisdom. Lord, I thank You that my discernment has increased. Father, in Jesus' name, I thank You for allowing me to see and perceive Your Kingdom. Father, I thank You for Your wisdom and understanding to know when to speak and when to hold back. Father, I thank You for

Your wisdom and discernment to know when to press forward and when to rest. Father, in Jesus' name, I thank You for Your wisdom with leading and walking by faith. In Jesus' name, I pray, amen.

### Prayer for Women's Health

Father, in Jesus' name, I thank You that You have blessed the women's reproductive system. Lord God, in Jesus' name, I call forth full restoration and health within the women's body. Lord God, I ask that You show me what foods I should and should not eat. Lord, I ask that You reveal anything that may be out of alignment. Father, in Jesus' name, I ask that You bring my womanly body into full alignment with Your Word and glory. Father, in Jesus' name, I declare that my womb is blessed. Father, I decree that every hormone is within Your balance. Father, I declare that my organs are blessed. Father in Jesus' name, I declare that my body is blessed and is in excellent health. Father, in Jesus' name, I thank You. Amen.

## Closing Declaration

**Declaration to abide in Christ**

I am confident in this: I am a Child of God. I am loved by the Almighty. He has called me beloved. He has called me the apple of His Eye. I will abide in Christ. Jesus said that if I abide in Him, then He will abide in me. Therefore, I know Jesus is with me. I am confident that God has me resting under the shadow of His wings.

He loves me, and I shall dwell in the House of the Lord forever. I shall have life abundantly. I am a child that seeks the Father. For I shall rest at that Father's feet. For the presence of the Lord is where my home is. I declare that I will abide in the presence of the Lord FOREVER!

*Psalm 91:1 – He who dwells in the secret place of the Most High shall abide under the shadow of the Almighty.*

**Declaration to be whole in Christ**

I am whole. I am wonderfully and fearfully made. Marvelous are Your works! I am complete. Through Christ, Jesus, I am perfect and lacking nothing. I am more than enough. I am loved. I have abundant peace. I am filled with Joy. I walk with confidence. I am free. I have the love of Christ within me. I walk in wholeness, for the Blood of Jesus has set me free.

## Closing Declaration

*Psalm 139:14 – I will praise You, for I am fearfully and wonderfully made; Marvelous are Your works, and that my soul knows very well.*

### Declaration to be bold in Christ

The righteous are bold as a lion. I am a fervent worshipper. I am filled with the Holy Ghost Fire. I am filled with the courage and faith of the Lamb. For I walk by faith and not by sight. I hold my trust in the Lord. Though darkness surrounds me, I will fear NO evil. I have the power of the Holy Spirit. I walk in the authority that is given by Christ Jesus. I speak with Holy Ghost audacity. I have faith to move mountains. I am confident that if God said it, then surely it will come to pass.

I shall wait upon the Lord.

I shall mount up on wings like eagles. I shall run and not be weary. I shall walk and not faint. I am more than a conqueror, and I will see the exceedingly and the abundantly over my life. – Selah.

*Proverbs 28:1 – The wicked flee when no one pursues, but the righteous are bold as a lion.*

*Armani D. White*

## *Salvation Prayer*

**Dear Heavenly Father,**

In Jesus' name, I repent of my sins. I ask that You forgive my sins and trespasses. Lord, I also ask that You help me acknowledge You in all that I do. Jesus, I ask that You come into my heart and be Lord over my life. Father, Your Word in Romans 10:9-10 says, 'that if I confess with my mouth the Lord Jesus and believe in my heart that YOU have raised Him from the dead, then I will be saved.' So, Father, with my mouth I confess and with my heart I believe that Jesus died on the cross for my sins and that You raised Him from the dead so that I may live. In Jesus' name, I pray, Amen.

Thank you for rescuing me from the powers of darkness. You have given me victory and dominion over my enemies. For this and much more, I give thanks to Jesus Christ, my Lord and Savior. Amen.

Since you said this prayer and have dedicated your life to Christ (or back) by faith, you are saved! I would love to hear of your great news and would love to help keep you accountable by inviting you to join our Discipleship program. Register at:

www.RiseMinistry.org/Discipleship

## Books by Armani White

You're More Than Enough

Owning your Purpose

♦

My Sweet Savior

'90 Day Devotional'

Building an Intimate Relationship with Jesus

♦

Prayer Tool

## Course

*Online Book Writing Course* – No More delay, Publish your book NOW! Visit us at: www.RiseMinistry.org/PublishNow

♦

*Discipleship Program* – If you desire to build an intimate relationship with Jesus and to know Him more, join our Discipleship Program. www.RiseMinistry.org/Discipleship

www.ingramcontent.com/pod-product-compliance
Lightning Source LLC
Chambersburg PA
CBHW051106160426
43193CB00010B/1334